# Rennie goe[illegible]

This is a Green Knight [illegible] and well-written story ab[illegible] job, incorporating up-to-date facts and figures, and helpful advice.

Seventeen-year-old Rennie Jordan wants only one thing in life: to work with horses. Despite opposition from her family, she joins the staff of Kingwood Riding School, where she fights to overcome her lack of confidence and stamina. She finds many problems at first, but the enjoyment and satisfaction of doing the only work she has ever wanted to do overcome all the difficulties.

'It will interest the many who have anything to do with horses and in particular any who hope to earn a living by caring for them. *Rennie Goes Riding* manages to entertain and at the same time to convey plenty of sound information.'
*The Times Educational Supplement*

*Other novels in this career series*

AIR HOSTESS ANN

MARGARET BECOMES A DOCTOR

THREE TOP SECRETARIES

Monica Edwards

# Rennie goes riding

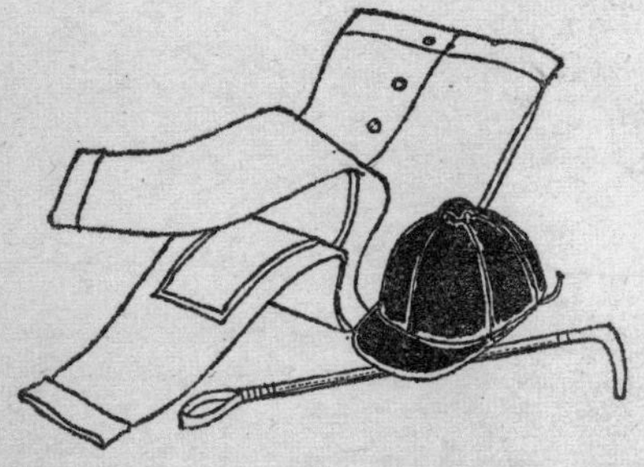

KNIGHT BOOKS

*the paperback division of Brockhampton Press*

SBN 340 04011 4

*This revised edition first published* 1968 *by Knight Books, the paperback division of Brockhampton Press Ltd, Leicester*

*Printed and bound in Great Britain by Richard Clay (The Chaucer Press) Ltd, Bungay, Suffolk*

*First published by The Bodley Head Ltd* 1956
*Second impression* 1961

*This book is sold subject to the condition that it shall not by way of trade or otherwise be lent, re-sold, hired out, or otherwise circulated without the publisher's prior consent in any form of binding or cover other than that in which this is published and without a similar condition including this condition being imposed on the subsequent purchaser*

# Contents

# 1 | A Real Interest

RENNIE JORDAN had really tried to make her hand write; but though it would pick up and hold a pen, it simply would not, could not, form one word. This kind of thing had happened to her several times in her seventeen years of almost continual ill health. Most often, as on this evening, it happened when she settled down in the quiet dining-room to do her homework. Once or twice it had happened at school, particularly now that she was older and not moving up with other girls of her own age.

Aunt Lucy took the view that a firmer line was all that was really necessary. Rennie could hear her now, perfectly clearly, discussing the matter with Mr Jordan in the sitting-room. It was funny how Aunt Lucy sometimes didn't think of shutting the door or lowering her voice – as if, perhaps, she thought that it might be good for Rennie to overhear some things for her own good. There was nothing new, however, in what Aunt Lucy had to say; and, as usual, Rennie's father listened in almost complete silence. Rennie could see him in her mind's eye, sitting before the usual pile of school exercise-books that awaited his correction, puffing patiently at his pipe and courteously waiting for Aunt Lucy to finish.

'Of course, the accident was quite a different matter, I grant you,' Aunt Lucy was saying in her brisk, intelligent voice; 'with the child being so young then, and conscious all the time she was buried under the house after the explosion, and with the injuries she had, poor mite. You can understand it's affecting her nerves, I suppose.'

Rennie could hear her father's pencil tapping quietly on the table. He was probably thinking of what a trial the Lower Fourth had been today, and of how he was to pay for a new bicycle for young Robin on a schoolmaster's meagre salary.

'But the car-crash was quite different,' stated Aunt Lucy. 'She was hardly hurt at all, let's face it; and though I know it must have been a severe shock to see her own mother killed, it's four years ago now, and time she pulled herself together and got over it.'

'It was Mary who really helped her more than anyone else, after the accident,' Rennie heard her father point out gently, still absently tapping.

'That's just it,' said Aunt Lucy emphatically; 'helped her too much, is what I think, Roy. She ought to have encouraged her to stand up for herself more. Well, look at her now. She hasn't got her mother any more to be a buffer for her, and she just lets go. Honestly, Roy, the child simply doesn't try. This business of saying she can't move her hands: even the doctor says it's only really psychological, and not physical at all. There's nothing wrong with her *hands*. The same when her knees give, and things like that. Have you noticed that it happens only when she finds things difficult? The whole thing is really only in her mind, that's what it is, and she ought to make more effort.'

Rennie heard her father murmur something that sounded like, ' "the dark, uncharted continent of the mind..." ', and then there was a rush of running steps in the hall and her young brother Robin came whirling in at the door.

'Oh, sorry! are you doing your homework still? I finished mine ages ago.' He was a very fair, very pink child of nine or ten, his pinkness plunging in at his collar and reappearing from under his shorts, at the knees.

'It's all right,' Rennie said. 'I hadn't properly started.'

'Oh, gosh! have your hands seized up again? Rotten chizz! I heard of a fellow who wrote a whole book with his feet. Have you tried using your feet? Or have they seized up, too?'

Rennie said, 'People can't write with their feet unless they've done it since they were small.' She got up and went over to open the window, leaning out into the late June evening.

'Your hands have come back!' Robin shouted cheerfully. 'You opened the window. Now you can do your homework and not get into a shozzle at school.'

Rennie stared at her brown hands, so strong and supple-looking, and flexed her fingers experimentally. Then she said, 'I can't. It's homework that does it to them.'

'Well, will you come out and have a game of French cricket, then?'

'I can't. Not when I haven't done my prep.'

'Oh, Rennie, you really are hopeless,' said Robin impatiently. 'It's always "can't" with you. Why don't you ever *try*?'

'You got that from Aunt Lucy,' said Rennie sadly.

'Well honestly, you are a bit of a case,' said Robin frankly. 'The only thing you do take any interest in is horses and riding, which Dad can't afford – and you wouldn't be much good at, anyway, the way you are – and because you can't have horses and riding, you won't take an interest in anything. Now I think the world's full of interesting things. Well, just think what it'd be like to have me moping about and all that, just because I can't have a plane and learn flying.'

Rennie furrowed her brow. Even when she was worried and anxious, which she often was, she still looked no more than fifteen, with her small, slight figure and straight, boyish hair. 'It isn't because of that. It's because – because I think that horses are the only thing I really could be any good at – until I'm better, I mean, and because they're the only thing that I really very much care about. I *have* tried other things, only perhaps you were too young to remember: the piano and dancing and tennis, and things like that.'

'And did you seize up?' Robin asked, with a small boy's curious interest.

'Sometimes,' said Rennie evasively. 'Anyway, I wasn't any good at them.'

Robin swung round on his heels to the door again, disappointed at this lack of medical detail. 'Oh, well, if you can't come out, I suppose you can't. And a lovely day like this! I'll go and see if Philip can.'

Rennie heard the cheerful thud of his shoes going down the hall again, and then, as though her aunt had awaited the moment, the brisk tap of her approaching heels.

'Rennie.'

'Yes, Aunt Lucy?'

'I've been talking to your father.'

Rennie looked at her, quietly waiting. She had a faint suggestion of Robin about her, as if she might have been a caricature of him: tall and fair and pink, but angular and crisply efficient, where he was still curved and attractively boyish.

'We think perhaps you might leave your homework again, and I will write Miss Foster a note.'

'Oh, thank you, Aunt Lucy!' Dear Aunt, Rennie thought wistfully. She did her conscientious best, even giving up her excellent job as matron of a girls' reformatory school in order to look after Rennie and Robin for her widowed brother-in-law. Rennie was sorry that she was always such a worry to her: she would so much have liked to be a credit; popular and clever at school, good at games, useful and cheerful in the house.

'But Rennie, dear.'

'Yes, Aunt Lucy?'

'Don't you think you really could try, now – make a real effort – to get over all this? Think of people like Douglas Bader, who didn't let losing both legs get him down; and that wonderful Helen Keller, born deaf, dumb, and blind, but overcame it all.'

Rennie twisted the ends of her tunic girdle, staring out of the window with clouded brown eyes.

'Daddy and the doctor and I all think that you would be better if you would take a real interest in something – *do* something with your hands, for example,' went on Aunt Lucy. 'Isn't there anything you would like to try? Modelling – we could get the clay – or skating, even? I'm told there's a good rink at Charterhill, but only roller-skating, I'm afraid. Or would you like to have a plot of garden of your own? Or another try at piano lessons?'

Rennie sighed a little, her brow furrowing up anxiously again. She wished that she could have pleased Aunt Lucy. 'I – I don't think so, thank you. At least, only horses. I d-don't think I should be any good at anything but horses. I don't even want to do anything, except with horses. I'm sorry, Aunt Lucy, really I am!'

This time Aunt Lucy sighed, but louder and less patiently than Rennie. 'Really, dear, I do think sometimes that you are almost deliberately difficult. Horses would be the worst possible thing for anyone in your nervous condition – and Daddy and the doctor both say the same thing. Even if we could afford for you to have riding lessons, it would be madness for us to do so. Horses are very dangerous and highly sensitive animals, my dear, and only people with the very strongest nerves are any good with them. I know; I had a few lessons myself when I was at school, and my instructor told me, "Think of the reins as telegraph lines, that carry your confidence or nervousness directly to your mount." You know perfectly well how nervous you would be, and your horse would know it, and there'd be an accident, and you'd be worse than ever, again.'

'All right, Aunt Lucy, dear.' Rennie smiled wanly. 'M-may I go for a walk? There's p-plenty of time before bed.'

'Yes, do, dear; it'll do you good. And Rennie – try not to

stutter, won't you? You were getting better at that, I thought.'

Rennie nodded mutely. She always stuttered if she tried not to. It was only when she did not think about it that the words came smoothly. It was the same with writing. She could write fluently for hours in her horsy notebook, copying things from library books and papers; it was only when she had to make a conscious effort that her hands went numb. She went out through the kitchen and back door, down through the little orchard and along the field path that led to Tom Pigram's place.

Tom was by way of being a retired groom, but, as he had once said to Rennie, the more he retired, the busier he became. Just now, he had a young chestnut colt belonging to a Colonel somebody, that he had taken for breaking and schooling. With any luck, she might see him working with the colt in the paddock where he had his old caravan and stable buildings. But it seemed that she was to have no luck this time, because just as she came round the corner of Withy Wood and in sight of the Pigram holding, she heard the staccato noise of his motor-cycle leaving the yard. He would be going to one of the Charterhill district stables where he 'obliged' by cleaning tack and clipping and trimming horses in his spare time. It was disappointing – but the chestnut colt would still be there. He was a darling, and Rennie was not afraid of him at all. He would come up to her in the field and snuffle for sugar or an apple, and he would lower his lovely head to be scratched gently behind his ears. She could see him now, grazing quietly against a high hedge that was spangled with wild roses. The slanting evening sun made his bright coat look like polished copper, and his mane moved like water as he tore at the summer grass and clover. His name was Templar, and Rennie called it as she walked across the field.

'Templar! Come on, old fellow; I've got something for you.'

The colt lifted his head, in one lovely smooth movement. All his movements were full of grace, and he came swinging towards her with his fluid walk, through clover humming with late bees.

'Not that pocket – the other one,' said Rennie as he whickered and nudged around her blazer to smell the sugar she had brought for him. She gave it to him on the flat of her palm, as the library books had taught her, so that her fingers should not get nipped; and then she gently rubbed his soft-whiskered muzzle, and stroked his neck and shoulder. The colt had been used to handling since his early days, and had not been bullied or shouted at, to make him afraid of man. He looked over Rennie's shoulder, carelessly slobbering on her collar: he gave a deep, contented sigh, pushing her clumsily and affectionately with his head and returned to grazing round her feet. Rennie played with his mane, plaiting a strand of it as she had seen in the books on horsemanship, and wondered whether all this delightful sense of confidence – which she never had anywhere else – would really leave her if she were on his back and not standing here in Tom Pigram's field beside him.

It would be wonderful just to try it, she reflected wistfully; but the colt was not properly broken yet; and even if he were, Tom was not here to see that she was all right and to hold him for her. And even if Templar were broken and Tom were here, she thought sadly, it still wouldn't be any use, because Templar didn't belong to Tom; and so, of course, Tom would never dream of letting anybody else do anything with him, to say nothing of trying to ride him.

It was then that the wild, exciting, dreadfully shocking thought struck her. Why shouldn't she take advantage of Tom's absence, and this quiet, lonely field, and the unlocked harness-shed, to find out for herself? The mere thought of this so shook her that she began to feel the old weakness at her knees again, as if she were going to kneel down. Sometimes, when this had happened, she *had* knelt down – just where she was, in the form-room or at home. But this time there was something else fighting inside her against the sudden weakness of her nerves – a genuine interest in the thing that she had set herself to do. Determinedly, if a little shakily, she began to walk towards the sheds.

# 2 | The Great Adventure

Tom Pigram was a trusting man, considering how hopeless was his old spaniel Joey as a watchdog: for, though the caravan door was locked, a window was open, and there were not even any keyholes on the sheds. Joey lay on his fat side, panting in the shade of his green kennel. He was not chained – he never was – but after half-rising to greet Rennie he quickly rejected this energetic idea and sank back again, apologetically whacking the yard-stones with his tail.

'Hallo, Joey; good dog!'

As she walked to the tack-room door she began to feel the first small wave of nervous anxiety lap over her. What would Joey do when she opened the door and went in? When she came out carrying a bridle? He had always been very friendly, in an exhausted sort of way, on the few occasions when she had met him before. But then Tom had been there, and Rennie had not been snooping in his sheds.

Her hand was shaking a little as she laid it on the catch, but Joe had lost all interest and had returned to his summer evening torpor. Rennie's breath went out in a long sigh of relief at this first difficulty dealt with, and she opened the door and stood staring at the collection of bridles, halters, rugs, saddles, and other stable equipment that was tidily arranged on the walls and bench and shelves inside. Which were Templar's? Had he, in fact, ever worn a proper bridle? When she had last watched Tom at work on the colt he had been long-reining him, but that had been more than a week ago, and Tom spoke then of planning to saddle and back him shortly.

Twisting her fingers nervously behind her back, Rennie pondered these things; and then decided not to risk a saddle at all. Not even a bridle, perhaps, because of the awful business of having to get the bit in Templar's mouth – especially if he had never worn one – to say nothing of making the bridle fit him, if she happened on one that wasn't his. She would ride him in a leather halter – a head-collar, as the books called it. Of course, without a bit she would have very little control; but then, with her small knowledge and total lack of experience, would she even have any control with a bit? Probably she would only ruin the colt's mouth altogether; so that a head-collar was really the best thing, after all. And if he broke away from her and galloped round the field, he wouldn't be trampling on reins and breaking an expensive bridle, either.

Reaching up, she lifted down a nice-looking head-collar, beautifully supple and cleaned and with shining brass buckles and D-ring, from which hung a flexible rope. She swung round to the door, anxious to get on with her plan before either she lost her nerve for it entirely or someone came along and stopped her. But Joey was now standing in the doorway, and he was lifting his droopy lips up over his teeth in a kind of half-hearted snarl. Rennie's heart gave a huge bump, and she stared at the dog uneasily for a moment; until suddenly she saw his stump slowly wagging and realized that it must be his idea of a warm-weather smile.

'Good dog, Joey,' she said again, and, grasping the head-collar very tightly, braced herself to walk out past him and into the sun and space of Templar's clover field again.

She had nothing left to give him this time, which made her anxiety twang back at her again – if only she had thought of all this in advance – but the colt was a kindly tempered horse and, after a preliminary hopeful whicker and snuffle, he gave up hoping and let her slip the head-collar up over his muzzle and buckle it on with fumbling, nervous fingers. At this point, he obviously expected to be led back to the stable, but Rennie looked around her and then led him to a water-tank that stood in a corner of the field. She would be able to mount from this, she decided.

The colt came freely, brushing along through the grass and bees and clover with his long, free stride, and Rennie felt grateful and encouraged, her sapping confidence slowly creeping back. After all, she told herself, he was a sweet-tempered horse and not likely to do anything deliberately to hurt her. If he should hurt her, it would be because he was frightened too – more frightened, perhaps, than she was – or because he was very young and playful and excitable. And supposing, she said to herself, facing the ultimate possibility, that he should kill her? Not, of course, intentionally, but because they were two young things who knew almost nothing, between them, about the way of a man with a horse. It could happen: it easily might: it had to other people. Well, let it, Rennie said to herself doggedly, coming up to the tank: there isn't really any use in going on living, the way I am: please, God, either let him kill me quickly, or let me ride him so that I know I can be better than I am.

The colt stood quietly at the tank when Rennie stopped him. He blew and pushed at the water with his muzzle as if to say, 'Thank you for bringing me along, but I really don't want any. Then he dribbled all down Rennie's blazer sleeve. She was wearing her school tunic, but its pleats were full enough for straddling. With a kind of desperate determination she stepped on to the corner of the tank, and then – glorious, terrifying thing to do – she had slithered on to Templar's back.

For a moment the colt was too surprised to do anything; and Rennie's heart had nearly stopped beating with the fright and wild excitement that was crashing round inside her. One brown hand clutched the head-rope and the other fastened itself tightly in his mane.

'G-good horse, Templar,' she said, and released her clutch on his mane for a moment to pat him reassuringly; but her teeth were chattering so hard that she stuttered, and suddenly she remembered: 'You will be nervous, and the horse will know it, and there'll be an accident, and you will be worse than before.'

Templar, too, had been thinking and had sized up the situation: he reacted by hunching his back and swishing his tail. Rennie sat tight, every muscle aching with nervous tension. Templar walked an uncertain step or two, his own powerful muscles rippling under Rennie's bare legs. She pulled a little on the head-rope and Templar snorted, shooting his sensitive ears backward. Then suddenly, with a shake of his head, he began to go sideways, crab-like. He stopped and pawed the ground. He made a small, tight circle of little springy steps, with his head down; and through the fog of fear in Rennie's mind there flashed the thought that this was because she was pulling him sideways with the head-rope. She slackened her hold on it a little, very cautiously, and Templar bounded forward. He was shaking his head again, and throwing it up and down. His back felt slithery and insecure under her as he swung faster down the field. His canter was very smooth and free, but to Rennie it was the most terrifying thing she had ever done. The air seemed to rush past her, and the tall hedge, hung with wild roses, to rush towards her madly like the bottom of a pit in a nightmare.

The colt had made himself frightened, and he was galloping now, and Rennie could feel herself slowly slipping sideways on the roundness of his back. She leaned desperately on the rope, but only pulled herself forward on the silky summer coat. Suddenly the hedge was high in front of her, and Templar stopped with all his hoofs dug into the turf, and Rennie shot over his head and into the middle of the hawthorn and the roses.

Somehow she pulled and scrambled and tore herself out. There was the chestnut colt, tranquilly grazing, the head-rope trailing by his side.

'Good horse, Templar,' Rennie said again, and somehow she was walking towards him. It was funny really, she thought, that she was walking in this ordinary way, because she hardly felt as if she were there at all, but rather as if she were floating in the air somewhere above herself and looking on with faint surprise and consternation. The colt allowed her to approach, eyeing her a little doubtfully but not moving away. She patted his neck uncertainly; and then suddenly she was aware again of the old, strong tide running in her of love for all horses, everywhere. It was a kind of unity, almost a sense of dedication; a knowing that all her life was ordained to be spent with and for horses, and that somehow it would all come to pass, because it was her firm vocation.

Rennie unbuckled Templar's head-collar and took it off. The colt gave a long, snorting sigh, as if relieved to be rid of it, and returned to the grasses and the clover.

Feeling as if she were not really awake at all, Rennie took the head-collar back to the shed and hung it carefully in its place. She said, 'Hullo, Joey,' to the spaniel, shut the door, and then walked home along the field path and through the orchard. But when she reached her own back door her knees gave way, and it was no good trying to make them straighten up and behave as good knees should do. They had brought her home, but now the strain of Rennie's great adventure was making its effect, and they gave up trying. Aunt Lucy found her there, kneeling on the doorstep, and called for Mr Jordan to help her. There was a great deal of fuss, of course.

'Where *have* you been, child? All scratched, and your tunic torn!'

'I – I fell in a hedge,' said Rennie evasively. Nothing, nothing, should make her tell about the colt. She had really ridden him once, and she would ride him again – and next time she would ride him better. She would use two ropes on the head-collar, or a bridle with the bit left out....

'Fell in a *hedge*? How on earth did you do that?' asked Aunt

Lucy suspiciously, putting a rug round Rennie's useless legs. She was always practical, even in sudden emergencies when so many people run about in circles.

'Leave her alone, Lucy; I should,' said Mr Jordan patiently. 'It doesn't really matter how she fell.'

'I'll get you some strong, sweet tea,' said Aunt Lucy. 'What a good thing Robin's in bed; this sort of thing is so bad for young children, I think.'

'I'd r-rather have the tea weak and with no sugar,' Rennie said, because that was the only kind of tea she liked.

'Strong and sweet's much better for your nerves,' said Aunt Lucy briskly, and went into the kitchen. 'And then early bed,' she called through the open door. 'I always sent my girls early to bed after any little upsets: there's nothing like it.'

Rennie's father sat quietly for a minute or so, puffing leisurely at his pipe. And then he said diffidently, for he disliked encroaching on the privacy even of youth, 'Did anything frighten you, Rennie? Everything all right?'

'I'm all right, Dad. Actually, I've had a w-wonderful time.'

'Just walking in the fields?'

'Just in the f-fields,' said Rennie. 'I'm sorry about my legs, Daddy.'

'Stupid old legs,' said Mr Jordan, as if she had been a small child. 'Never mind, they'll grow out of it. Here comes your tea.'

# 3 | No Permission

THAT night, Rennie woke the whole house up, screaming from the dark centre of her old nightmare. It took Aunt Lucy and Mr Jordan five minutes to convince her that she was not pinned with her mother under a burning car, but safe in her own bed at home.

For a long time Rennie lay awake after that. There was a great deal to think about, and she was young to be faced with problems of a magnitude that would have baffled most grown-ups. She understood her own nervous illness far less than did the doctors and specialist who treated her – and had been able to do so little to make her well – but she knew that sudden strains would bring on breakdowns, and that in seeking to ride the chestnut colt she was subjecting herself to quite enormous strains on her nervous system.

Everything awful seemed to have happened today – apart from the one glorious highlight of riding the colt. There had been first the failure of her hands, and then of her knees, after weeks of having hardly any trouble with them: her stutter had come back, and now the nightmare. And Rennie knew that homework was not responsible for all of it.

If she went on with her plan of riding the colt again on other evenings when Tom was out on part-time jobs, would she end in curing herself as she hoped, or would she crock herself up completely? People sometimes talked of kill-or-cure remedies: well, this obviously was one, and she had to decide now whether she was going to take the risk. It really all depended on whether she was right or not, in thinking that only through horses could she find again any confidence in herself and in a worrying world. She had tried, of course, to arrive at the same result by the normal way of having riding lessons, but she hadn't a forceful enough character to convince Aunt Lucy and her father that it really was the only thing and that she believed she could do well at it. If health was, as people said, worth more than any money or hazard, her riding lessons might have been worth all their cost. Well, then, was riding the colt worth any cost or hazard as well? The possible cost, say, of a final breakdown in her health, supposing that her experiment should fail?

Deciding again that it was worth even that, Rennie went to sleep as the summer dawn came greyly through her window to a shout of waking blackbirds.

Two evenings later she was riding the colt again. This time, Joey hardly troubled to lift one eyelid as she went into the tack-room for Templar's head-collar, and he was openly snoring in the shadow of his kennel when she was tying on the second rope – a piece of clothes-line that she had brought with her, hoping Aunt Lucy would not miss it. She had extra chunks of carrot in her pocket, too, this time, and Templar came willingly enough to nuzzle at her blazer, though it hadn't occurred to her to hide the head-collar behind her back. He really was the sweetest-natured horse, Rennie said to herself as he stood peacefully crunching while she fastened the shiny brass buckles. It was absurd, the way her hands were shaking again, as though he were savage and vicious and bad. She supposed it was really because he was in fact dangerous, owing to being scarcely half-broken, and because she was anxious too that she should not spoil him by her own inexperience. She was also troubled about the rights and wrongs of taking him without permission. But, in a sense, Rennie was fighting for life; and the only full life that she could see was through horses, and no permission was given for her to learn to handle horses. So Rennie fought her conscience down and rode without permission and secretly.

This evening the colt began by going very nicely. There was no sideways crab-walk, no pawing and circling. He set off quickly and smoothly in his long, swinging walk round the field, and the only things that he did to frighten Rennie were the old headshaking and, again, a horrifying series of half-bucks which almost sent her straight over his shoulder. But she pushed herself back by his mane and gripped with her knees as she had read that one should do, talking quietly and reassuringly to the colt all the time, but she wished that she didn't feel so turned-to-water terrified, since her fear would surely be running down the rope reins and passing on to Templar.

It was strange how sensitive horses were. The colt was already growing more excited, as he had done the time before. Either he was really affected by her nervousness or he simply worked himself up as he went. Whichever way it was, he was cantering now, and without a saddle to help her Rennie only hauled herself forward when she tried to pull him up. Perhaps the sound of his own drumming hoofs stirred him more, but the next thing was that the colt was galloping again, just as before, and there was nothing at all that Rennie could do to stop him. This time there was no tall, thick hedge rushing at her, because they were going round and round the field, and Rennie began to wonder in a fatalistic sort of way what the end of it would be. If the colt ran himself down, would she have 'broken his wind', as the books put it, and ruined him for life? Or could she even stay on for as long as that? It would take very little to unseat her at this pace. She wondered what it would be like to hit the ground from a gallop, and suddenly her mind was full of remembering what it had been like to see the lorry coming into them, when her mother had been driving that day. Rennie's hands, and then her knees, went suddenly limp. They were passing the water-tank when she fell, and her arm and shoulder hit the iron side of it before she slumped into the grass.

The colt slowed down and came to a halt, blowing a little, his shining side lifting. Then he settled down to graze again, with the rope-reins trailing, and it was more than an hour before Tom Pigram came home and found the state of things in his paddock. But Joey was still lying snoring and twitching in the yard, though the bees had gone from the clover.

After Tom had got over the shock of finding that it was Rennie, of all the impossibly unlikely people, who had been riding the colonel's colt in secret, he began to be characteristically brisk and practical. You must be very careful how you move people after an accident, he knew well, because of making unknown injuries much worse. But you didn't leave them lying in a hunch. Gently, the old groom straightened Rennie out, noting the limpness of her left arm as he did so. You had to keep accident cases warm, because of shock. So Tom Pigram ran on his stiff, thin bow-legs to fetch a blanket from his van, but his natural horse-sense caused him to stop and take off Templar's head-collar on his way, because the colt might tread on the trailing ropes and frighten or hurt himself.

'I *thought* that head-collar'd been mucked about with, two days gone,' he muttered to himself as he threw it into the tack-room. 'So it aren't the first time, neither.'

Then, grabbing a grey, hairy blanket from his bunk, he was quickly stilting back again across the paddock. His legs were only made for riding, and he had bad feet besides, and in any case he never reckoned to run as fast as this, if at all.

Having covered up his patient, the next thing was to think what to do about her. Neither he nor Rennie's father had a telephone, nor had either of them a car. Well, there was always the gamekeeper's cottage at the edge of the wood, Tom decided, and started running again. With any luck, Albert would be in for his supper, and they could rig up a pole stretcher with their jackets and carry her home. But Albert, said his stout wife, was unaccountably late. She supposed he must have come across a bad lot in the wood.

'Then, I'm sorry, mam, but I count you'll have to come yourself,' said Tom urgently, 'for it's no time to sit around waiting, and her unconscionable there with the colt in the paddick.'

All in a fluster, and protesting softly to herself, the gamekeeper's wife was chivvied into putting Albert's supper back into the oven, with a note on the table explaining her absence, after which she was further chivvied into finding two jackets of her husband's and two clothes-props, shutting up her cottage and making what speed she could with Tom back across the fields to his holding. She was as much handicapped by her weight and girth as Tom was by his feet and his shins. Together, like a giraffe and a hippopotamus flying before a bush fire, they puffed and wheezed and thumped and stilted and sweated through the quiet fields, followed by seven mildly curious cows across the whole length of one pasture.

Tom himself made the stretcher in his yard, with the two poles thrust through the sleeves of the two inside-out jackets, which were firmly buttoned up and finally roped for safety. He had learned to do this in the war years, and was now proud to think that he had not forgotten. With the creaking help of Albert's wife, who could only bend from the hips, he got Rennie comfortably installed upon the stretcher, and the pathetic party set out along the field path to her home.

The shock of this arrival on Aunt Lucy and Rennie's father was very great, because there had been no warning at all, except the slow advance of the stretcher up the garden-path. And Tom was not a particularly lucid explainer, and Albert's wife really knew almost nothing whatever about the matter and was as anxious for details as anybody else. Even Tom could only speculate, guessing with an improbable surmise at what had happened, and why. So that it was not until the next morning, when Rennie was conscious and considered fit to talk about it, that anything much was known at all.

She was in Charterhill Hospital now, which was fortunate for her because it did at least protect her from the brunt of Aunt Lucy's shocked and worried feelings. Rennie was shocked and worried enough herself, after first her accident and then the general anaesthetic in the hospital, and was in no state to be surrounded by the troubled feelings of anyone else. The nurses were just right – impersonal, serene, and quietly cheerful. No one worried Rennie at all, and she had nothing to do but start the long, slow process of recovering from a broken arm and collarbone and two cracked ribs.

Aunt Lucy was not unduly upsetting when she came to the hospital the next afternoon; perhaps partly because she had been gently warned by the Sister and Rennie's father, and partly because she was a sensible woman, if she wasn't very understanding of difficult people. Rennie's father asked her no questions at all, but brought her some peaches and grapes and apples that must have cost him his tobacco money for a month, a pile of her old horse-books, and her ball-point pen and horsy notebook: 'Because it isn't your right arm, luckily, and you may like to do some writing when you're better.'

Robin was not able to visit her because children under twelve were not allowed, but he sent her five toffees that he had left over from Saturday, and a little note, and a drawing of a farm horse with very hairy legs and a tail done up in a bun with straw and ribbons.

Aunt Lucy brought Rennie's cod-liver-oil-and-malt, and her vitamin B tablets ('so good for the nerves') and, with a flash of real inspiration, a pile of old *Geographical Magazines* that she had found in a second-hand bookshop on her way to the hospital. Trying valiantly not to say anything upsetting, she yet felt that she had to set her mind at rest as to what exactly Rennie had been doing in Tom Pigram's paddock, and why.

'I was riding the colt.' Rennie fiddled with her horsy notebook, turning the pages with her sound right hand.

'But Rennie, he isn't properly broken-in, surely?'

'I know.'

'Tom didn't say that you could, did he, dear?'

'No. I – I did it just to see if I could. And because – in a way – I sort of had to.'

'Well!' Aunt Lucy was too shocked about the whole thing to take it in properly at all. 'At least it will have done one good thing, dear. You'll know now that we were right when we said horse-riding wouldn't be any good to you. We did warn you, pet, but I suppose you had to find out for yourself.' She straightened Rennie's blue bed-cover and tidied the magazines into a neater pile on her locker.

Rennie said nothing, but stared across the private room that she had been given until she was considered fit to stand the bustle of a general ward.

'And when you come home,' went on Aunt Lucy comfortingly, 'we needn't have any more talk about horses at all, need we, now that you know it really isn't possible. I was saying to your daddy, I thought perhaps you'd like to have a puppy of your own, when you're better? How would that be, dear?'

Rennie said nothing for a minute or two, so that Aunt Lucy was beginning to repeat it all, and then she said in a small tired voice: 'Thank you very much, Aunt Lucy; but it wouldn't really be the same. I'm so sorry. But I don't think that I particularly want to get better if there won't be any horses.'

Aunt Lucy was deeply troubled. To think that, after all that had happened, the child should persist in her passion to learn about horses! One would have thought that, reasonably, she would never want to hear the word spoken again. What on earth was to be done? She wanted Rennie to be well and happy again, tiresome child though she often was. In fact, Aunt Lucy would have given much to see this frail but tenacious-charactered niece of hers as well and happy and boisterous as Robin was. With a tiny sigh of bafflement, she said kindly, 'Well, we must see what can be done about it,' and changed the subject to talk of Robin's coming sports day and what she should wear for it.

Aunt Lucy was a woman of her word. Before she left the hospital she had contrived to talk with Rennie's doctor, who had been visiting some of his patients and was still in the building. On her way home, later in the morning, sitting in the bus with a basketful of shopping on her knee, Aunt Lucy pondered over some recalled phrases from the doctor's conversation.

'But we must remember that the horse she was riding was only half-broken....'

'The strain she put on herself must have been very severe: really it's remarkable that she hasn't brought on a complete nervous collapse....'

'I don't honestly think that there is any point in her returning to school next term, do you?'

'In cases of Rennie's kind, we must realize that she may in fact be right when she says that there is only one way in which she can overcome her illness....'

'Of course, I do understand the money problem; I think that teaching is quite one of the most ill-paid professions in this country. Has Rennie a post-office savings account? She has twenty pounds? Then my advice to you, and to her father, Miss Ford, is to let her draw it all out – or as much as she needs – and spend the lot on proper riding lessons. There are one or two good establishments around Charterhill, I believe. Oh, and, Miss Ford, I should tell Rennie about it as soon as you can. These things all help with recovery, you know.'

Aunt Lucy stared through the window at the rushing summer leaves of the roadside, and thought regretfully to herself: a lifetime's savings! meant to give her a real start in life ... the first sixpence put in on the day that she was born.... But what was the use of having a start in life, if you hadn't any real life to start? Aunt Lucy thought about her own savings book. In hers there was much more than twenty pounds; but then, she had been saving for much longer, now, than Rennie had. She had been saving against her old age. She was nearer fifty than forty already, and getting a bit stiff in her joints when the wind was damp.

As the bus bumped swaying down the long hill into Baybridge, she began deliberately to weigh her age in the balance with Rennie's youth; and Aunt Lucy made her decision.

# 4 | Plans for Rennie

RENNIE's recovery was quicker than anyone would have believed possible. Her doctor said that it was because she now had something to live for.

'But she always had her father and Robin and me,' said Aunt Lucy, a little wistfully, looking pinker and more angular than ever.

'It was only half a life,' said the doctor, 'until she could teach herself how to live it. Now, we hope, she will soon be able to do so – because certainly no one else can.'

Aunt Lucy, though strongly disapproving, stood by the promises that she had made to Rennie and to herself. She began by walking along to Tom Pigram's place one afternoon, when Robin and his father were both at school in their different capacities, and found him unsaddling the colt in his yard, with the spaniel Joey lying prostrate by his kennel.

At first, Tom was rather unbending, being under the impression that Miss Ford might somehow be holding him to blame for Rennie's exploits. But she soon smoothed over this unpromising start by waiting calmly until Templar had been returned to his field, and then gently apologizing, for Rennie, for the liberties she had taken. In five minutes Tom and Aunt Lucy were getting on like grass in May, and he had said that he wouldn't dream of mentioning the matter to the Colonel, since the colt was as good and sound as ever, anyhow, and why worry the old gentleman? Aunt Lucy had expanded warmly about the anxiety dear Rennie was, and took full advantage of a totally new listener to the accident and car crash stories, gradually working round to the riding-school idea, though typically saying nothing at all about her own selfless decision in the matter of the money.

'Well now, Mam,' said Tom, leaning comfortably on the tack-room door-post, 'I might be able to help a bit there, in a manner of speaking like; me going to several stables by way of part-time work, see. There's old Tom Bushell's place – he's got one or two real nice ponies there; and there's Mr and Mrs Robinson, what have their stables at the Rainbow; and then Miss Brandon, out at Kingwood. Now she would be the one – that's right, mam – you couldn't do better. Not expensive, neither, as things go now,' he added when Aunt Lucy tentatively mentioned cost per hour. 'And she's a nice quiet lady, Mam. You know, the sort that gives confidence to a nervous learner, like.'

'She does sound the very thing,' agreed Aunt Lucy thoughtfully. 'Has she some really safe horses, too? We couldn't possibly risk another accident with Rennie, now.'

'Well, now,' said Tom, extending four stubby fingers and a thumb, and ticking them off one by one with his other hand, 'there's Flossie, she's a nice steady mare, she is; and then Brown Jane, and Julia – steady as a rock; and then there's old Hallmark – the pride of Miss Brandon's heart is old Hall. Had him seventeen year, she has, and he never put a foot wrong. But look, Mam, me kettle's boiling fit to bust on this stove here. I put it on fer cleaning me tack, but you wouldn't say no to a good cup of tea, I reckon?'

Aunt Lucy didn't say no. In fact, she was a few minutes late home to get tea on for Robin and his father, who would shortly be arriving on their bicycles from school. But she knew a whole lot more about her plans for Rennie, now, and was able to lay them before Mr Jordan, almost complete, except for Miss Brandon's own co-operation.

'Well, you can forget it all, Lucy, my dear,' said Mr Jordan, with sudden stubbornness. 'If you think Rennie and I are going to let you scatter your life's savings . . .'

There followed a spirited argument, in which young Robin lost interest when he found that he wasn't allowed to take part and make his own suggestions for the spending of Aunt Lucy's savings; so he finished his tea and went out and left them to it. And in the end it was stiffly agreed that Aunt Lucy and Rennie should pay equal halves of all the cost, and Aunt Lucy left the washing-up to wait in the sink while she went to write a long letter to Miss Brandon of Kingwood Riding School. In it she explained carefully the long history of Rennie's illness, and her need to 'find herself' again through learning to manage horses. She said little about money, except that it was very limited, and added that Rennie was strong and healthy and sensible and would do as she was told.

Miss Brandon's reply came two days later, and so filled Aunt Lucy with pleasant excitement in the success of her plans that she took it straight to the hospital the same afternoon to show Rennie.

Rennie was up, now, and due to come home within the week, and was looking better than she had looked since before the car-crash. She was in the garden of the hospital, with other convalescing patients, and she and Aunt Lucy read the letter among the roses on the hospital terrace.

'From what you tell me,' Miss Brandon had written, 'it seems that what Rennie really wants is not only to learn to ride but also to handle and work with horses.'

'She's right!' said Rennie eagerly. 'I hadn't really thought that far, myself, but it's what I do want to do.'

'I wondered,' went on the letter, 'whether she would care to come and stay here for a while, helping us about the stables in exchange for daily riding lessons? I should have to make a small charge for her keep, of course, but this plan would save her the daily journey out to Kingwood, and would be cheaper than a direct charge for lessons, while giving her the opportunity to be with horses all the time.'

'Oh, Aunt *Lucy*!' cried Rennie, her eyes suddenly shining in a way Aunt Lucy had never seen before.

'But wait a minute, dear,' said Aunt Lucy hastily, not wanting her to build up hope too high. 'Miss Brandon says, very sensibly, that she suggests a month's trial on both sides.... See' – she put a finger on the place – ' "so that if Rennie finds the work too tiring or difficult, or we find that she doesn't fit in happily with us, either she or I can terminate the agreement at the end of the month. I should add," ' went on Aunt Lucy, reading aloud, ' "that from what Tom Pigram has told me about Rennie's enterprise with his colt, I haven't very much doubt about her settling in with us here." '

'Does she mean doubt that I will fit in, or won't fit in?' Rennie asked, suddenly anxious.

'That you will fit in – silly!' said Aunt Lucy, smiling pinkly.

'Good old Tom!' said Rennie happily. 'It will be nice to see him in the evenings. Aunt Lucy, there won't be anything at all to pay for riding lessons, now! Just think of it – only my keep. When can I go to Kingwood? Next week?'

Aunt Lucy hedged. 'We must see what the doctor says, dear.' She sighed a little and added, 'I expect we shall miss you – your Daddy and Robin and I.'

Rennie squeezed her bony arm affectionately. 'You needn't. I'll come back and see you on my days off. And you'll all come and see me, too, sometimes, won't you?'

'Of course, dear,' said Aunt Lucy, and then added practically, 'Well now, we'd better start thinking about clothes. You haven't got one thing that'll do, and that's a fact.'

'Except my underwear and pyjamas,' said Rennie happily. 'We'll have to have a shopping day, Aunt Lucy. D'you suppose my savings will stretch to it?'

'They won't have to,' said Aunt Lucy firmly, 'nor for your

keep. I'm not going to be done out of the pleasure of having some finger in this affair, if it's only buying your clothes. And your father will pay for your keep, just the same as he'd be doing if you were at home.'

'Some day, soon, I'll be earning money and paying for my own keep,' said Rennie gravely; 'and doing it with horses.'

'Here comes your tea, dear,' said Aunt Lucy.

The doctor pronounced that Rennie should be fit for reasonable work in another three weeks' time. The days did not drag so intolerably as she had feared, because there were so many exciting things to fill them with; such as buying her clothes – jodhpurs, jerseys, jacket, and a riding-mackintosh – and watching Tom Pigram school Templar, or clean his tack while talking to her about Kingwood and the Colonel and horses he had known. Then there was the wonderful day when she visited Kingwood Riding School for the very first time, looking at everything with the wondering kind of eyes that try to realize how very familiar will strange things and people and horses soon become.

Miss Brandon was in a spare loose-box, feeding a Cairn bitch that had puppies, when Rennie and her family arrived on a fine Saturday afternoon. She straightened herself, an empty feed-bowl in her hand, and smiled at them all. At once a feeling of quiet confidence slipped into Rennie's mind. She had an impression of someone who would be as stinting with blame as she would be with praise; who would get a great deal done without apparent fuss and flurry, and would most probably never even raise her voice: and this was not a bad summary of the Kingwood Riding School proprietor's character. She welcomed them all in a quiet, almost detached way, and said to young Robin, who was squatting to stare at the puppies:

'Her name's Puffin, and she's very proud of her children, for all that they're not pure-bred Cairns. But sometimes she gets a bit tired of nursery life and comes round with one of us for a bit.'

'Are there more than one of you?' asked Robin, looking round.

'Oh, yes; there's Ann, who comes and helps me in the mornings; and Sally, who lives here, just as Rennie will. I expect you'll see Sally later. She's out at the moment with four children on a ride.' She turned and smiled a little at Rennie. 'You'd like to see some of the horses, I'm sure. And after that we'll look at the house and your room, and then I hope you'll all stay and have tea with me.'

The only real nervousness that Rennie had left was in meeting those wonderful people, Ann and Sally. She was absolutely sure that they would despise her for knowing so little, and she wondered how much they knew about her illness and whether they would despise her for that, too. Meanwhile, it was lovely to be following Miss Brandon out to the paddocks, and listening to the satisfactory way that her father and Aunt Lucy were getting on with her. Robin, too, was displaying an astonishing interest in everything, for one whose only passion was aircraft.

'The horses are all out at grass now,' Miss Brandon was saying, 'but very soon we shall be getting the hunters up, so that we can get them into condition for the season, and as the autumn goes on we fetch more of the horses in. By the Christmas holidays we usually have ten or a dozen in all the time, and often another half-dozen or so in at nights.'

'And then there really is some work to do!' said Rennie's father, grinning at Rennie.

'There really is,' agreed Miss Brandon, with her slight smile. 'It's always harder in the winter; but the working days are often longer in the summer, because of evening rides.'

They were walking down the double row of empty loose-boxes, through a roomy, cobbled yard and out to the tree-shadowed lane that led to the fields and Kingwood village.

Aunt Lucy praised the beauty of the Hampshire countryside, and Robin shouted with delight to find that they were being followed, not only by Puffin but by a friendly ginger cat as well. Rennie's father was talking with Miss Brandon about schools' riding classes, but Rennie alone said nothing, because she was so occupied in absorbing impressions. There had been that exciting glimpse into the tack-room, lined with saddles and bridles and with a glass case quite full of rosettes on the wall; there was the mounting-block in the yard, and another range of stables stretching into the trees.

'The pony stables,' Miss Brandon explained. 'We keep hay and straw and bantams as well as ponies in there. We're really very lucky to have such good buildings. They used to be the stables and farm buildings of the big house behind the trees, there. It was Kingwood House before the war, and now it's Kingwood School, and we have their boys for riding classes, which is a great help, because they pay a flat rate every term, so that we don't lose if the weather is too bad for them to come.'

'And is that your house, over the main stable block?' Aunt Lucy asked, looking back over her shoulder as they went along the lane.

Miss Brandon said it was, and that it had been adapted very well and conveniently, though there was still a trap-door down from her sitting room into the stables, relic of the days when it had been a hay-loft. 'Children love it, of course,' she said. 'I once put half a dozen very slippery small boys in there while I was getting some tea for them in the kitchen, but I lost them all down the trap into the stables!'

'Do you really have to go up all those wooden steps to your house?' Robin asked enviously. 'It must be fun – like living in a tree-house.'

Miss Brandon said that it wasn't quite such fun when you were feeling your way down on a dark winter's evening with a tray of tack-room tea: or even back up to the house at nine o'clock, after a long day's hunting followed by cleaning twelve muddy hunters and all their saddles and bridles: but she had that slight smile of hers, which suggested that she took most things as she found them.

'Now, there are some of the horses,' she said, as they rounded a corner hidden by trees. 'And a few of the ponies in the field on the other side. We have fields all over the place, and they are not all as handy as these two.'

She stopped and leaned on a gate looking into a wide, rolling field with park-like trees about it. At once, two horses lifted their heads and stared at her, though the others grazed on indifferently.

'My old Hallmark and Barbemusche,' Miss Brandon said. 'I've had dear old Hallmark almost ever since I left school; and now he's twenty-one and the Grand Old Man of the stables. The chestnut is Barbemusche. I'm very fond of him, and I think he's really fond of me, in his way, but he's a funny sort of horse. Not one for you to handle, Rennie,' she added with a smile. 'I think someone must have embittered him in his youth, poor old fellow.'

'Which is the one that looks just like an Edwardian carriage-horse?' Rennie asked, with her hands on the gate-post.

'Oh, that's the Dark Stranger! He does look rather dignified, I suppose! He had to have his tail docked because someone left a tail-bandage on too long and too tightly. That was before we had him. But he's a good cob really: he's won children's jumping more than once, as well as being a very reliable hunter. I remember at one gymkhana, he had to jump-off against himself, because two of our children were riding him and they tied for first place! But he's a moody sort of horse.'

'Which are Flossie and Julia and Brown Jane?' Aunt Lucy asked, remembering Tom's recommendations, but Miss Brandon said that they were all out carrying three old ladies. 'The little skewbald is Mermaid; she's a very nice ride; you'll like her, Rennie. And the spotted horse – he's almost an Appaloosa – is Jester. He goes well for a good rider.'

Robin said, 'Can we look at the ponies, please?' and climbed down from the gate.

'Over to the other side, then. There are four in that field – Walnut, Pixie, Jenny Wren, and Shamus. The ones that are out with Sally are Cobweb, Gingersnap, Brandysnap, and Acorn, and she's riding a cob called Spindle. Which leaves Snowcloud, Tittlemouse, and Jingle in the field beyond the school.'

'I shall never remember them all,' said Rennie, 'or know them one from another. Especially the ones that look so much alike.'

'You will,' said Miss Brandon serenely. 'I knew a shepherd, once, who looked after five hundred sheep. He said he knew every one by sight, and he did, too. They have all sorts of differences.'

'Like the Chinese people,' said Mr Jordan. 'They may look exactly alike to us, unless we've lived among them; but the fact is that we look exactly alike to them, too.'

'Yes; and just the same with horses, it's living with them that makes the difference,' said Miss Brandon. 'Now come and see the house and have a quiet cup of tea before the riders come home. It isn't very wonderful indoors, I'm afraid, as we have to do it all ourselves with only a woman in the mornings – my nice Mrs Waddy; she comes all the way from Charterhill – but it's warm and clean, and tea's tea wherever you have it!'

'I wish,' said Robin unexpectedly as they turned back down the lane, 'that *I* could learn to ride, too. Not that it would be half such fun as aeroplanes, but I think it *would* be fun, all the same.'

'Well, don't despair,' said Miss Brandon, peering round for Puffin and the tom-cat. 'You never know.'

# 5 Everyone Has to Start Sometime

Rennie looked at her jodhpurs and jacket where they lay on her bed waiting to be packed. They were only ready-made ones, because of being so much cheaper, but they were very nice and fitted her quite well, except for being a little roomy round the waist. There were also a pair of corduroy slacks, which Miss Brandon had suggested for stable work, and two strong, ribbed pullovers in brown and blue. Aunt Lucy had added a pair of string gloves and the riding-mack, and Rennie's father had presented her with a crash-cap and a cane. Robin had found a tie-pin that he decided he could spare for her, and Rennie bought herself two ties to go with it.

It was all quite wonderful, and she found it almost impossible to believe that school was really finished for ever, and that she was feeling better than she had felt for years, and was, this very day, about to start a whole month of living actually at a riding-school. Perhaps, if things went well, it would be for much more than a month . . . even years . . .

'I should put all the heavy things in the bottom,' said Aunt Lucy; and then suddenly lapsing into her other aggravating self, 'and Rennie, dear, try to remember that this is your one big chance, and do your best not to stutter, or drop things, or to shout out at night if you have bad dreams. Miss Brandon won't take as kindly to broken nights, I daresay, as your father and I have done; especially after a hard day with the horses. And if you should have much trouble with your knees or hands, dear, it might be best to come straight home and forget all about the riding. After all, that would be better than another bad accident, wouldn't it?'

'I'll be all right, Aunt Lucy, dear,' said Rennie patiently. 'I don't need labels on these cases, do I, just to Kingwood?'

'What an idea!' said Aunt Lucy. 'Supposing you left them on the bus, child?'

Rennie's whole family came to see her off at the bus stop after lunch, because there was no school for Robin and his father now that August had begun.

'Be sure to write at least once a week, dear,' Aunt Lucy was saying as Rennie gazed down the road for the bus.

'Take care of those broken bones for a bit,' said Mr Jordan; 'and remember I'm still here to be a buffer if you want me, however independent you may feel!'

'Don't worry, Daddy! I'll be all right,' Rennie said. 'I may even be seeing you next week-end, if I get a half-day.'

'May I come and help in the stables, sometime, when I get my new bike?' Robin asked. 'I'm old enough to be jolly useful, now.'

'Perhaps. I'll let you know. Here comes the bus. Good-bye, everybody, and thank you a thousand times for everything!'

'I could carry buckets of water,' Robin shouted above the noise of the bus, 'and groom ponies, and . . .'

'I'll see what I can do,' Rennie called, waving from the platform. 'Good-bye, good-bye!'

Two minutes later it seemed as if the whole of her childhood had been cut away with a knife, and she was leaving it behind her in Baybridge. She knew that she could not be leaving behind all the weary illness that had been such a large part of it, because illness of that kind was slow and difficult to cure. But she was full of a great hope that, from now on, the cure was beginning.

'No one can do any more for you, except only yourself,' her doctor had said when she left hospital. But Rennie believed that, without ever lifting a finger to do so, or being anything but herself, Miss Brandon could help, and that the horses could help.

The only thing that really worried her still was the morning stable-help, Ann. Sally was different. They had all met Sally after tea at Kingwood Stables, when she had ridden in grinning cheerfully and amiably with all her clattering, laughing pupils on their ponies. Sally was not the hypercritical sort. She didn't even look bristlingly efficient, and had dropped a bridle in the mud when she was beset by ponies being turned back into their field. But the mysterious Ann was yet to be seen. She was much older than Sally, Rennie knew, and was doubtless full of frightening efficiency, and therefore quite unable to help despising a nervous case who was also a total novice and lacking confidence as well. She might even be wearing make-up. Rennie couldn't be absolutely sure whether Sally had been wearing it, but if Ann and Sally did, then Rennie would too, despite the expense. But one thing she would not do for anybody, and that was change her hair style. She liked her floppy, straight, brown hair as it was, cut short in its pudding-basin style that suited her face and her riding-clothes. And after all, though she was seventeen, she didn't look it. Sally's hair was wild and frizzyish, and was probably natural. But Ann's, Rennie was quite certain, would be the last word, such as would look correct with stock and bowler. And her jodhpurs would have been made for her, and her jackets (she would have two) would fit her waist as if she had been poured into them. She might even be engaged to be married, and stop talking about it every time Rennie came in sight because of her being too young to understand.

These anxious speculations occupied Rennie until the bus stopped at the Kingwood turning, a mile or so before Charterhill. She was already on the platform and pulling her cases out from under the stairs before the conductor rang the bell. Miss Brandon had said that she would meet the bus with her little car, but there was no one in sight when Rennie stepped down on to the verge with her luggage. She watched the bus vanish down the hill, wondering whether she should start to walk, and then suddenly heard the quick sound of a trotting pony coming up the hilly lane from Kingwood. The trotting slowed to a walk now – where the hill was steep, that would be, Rennie decided – and then broke into trotting again; and suddenly a small black pony with a blaze came swinging round the bend, pulling a little painted tub-cart. Inside the cart was a sunburnt, wind-blown young woman with her jersey sleeves rolled up. Her shirt collar was open, and there was, plainly to be seen, straw in her reddish curly hair. Pulling up the pony, she began to turn him neatly in the lane, at the same time opening the little rear door of the tub-cart.

'You must be Rennie,' she was saying, with a quick smile. 'I'm Ann, and I've come to meet you because Miss Brandon's talking to a new client. Can you push your cases into the middle – up on end, I think – and then get in too?' She reached the hand that wasn't holding the reins, to help with the luggage, and it was a strong, squarish brown hand with two pieces of sticky plaster on it and the nails cut short.

'Shall I slam the door?' Rennie asked, scrambling after her cases.

'No, it isn't like a car-door; it shuts like this. Would you like to drive Shamus home?'

Rennie's eyes opened very wide. 'I couldn't possibly. I never have. I'm afraid I've never even ridden properly.'

Ann grinned again. She was always grinning, and whenever she did so her eyes crinkled up at the corners. 'Everyone has to start sometime.' She handed over the reins, and Rennie took them doubtfully. 'Really we ought to change places if you're driving, but it'd be too complicated dodging the cases. You've nothing to worry about with Shamus; he drives himself. Just keep a feel on the reins and he'll take us straight home. That's the idea. The only thing is, don't let him trot downhill.'

For about five minutes Ann talked on quickly and cheerfully about Shamus, and how he had come from Ireland, and hated men, so that they thought he must have been ill-treated by a man at some time; and what a good hunter he was, and how useful for taking poles to the gymkhana field in his trap. But Rennie only half-listened because she was so intent on this new experience. After a while she found confidence enough to say, 'It's much nicer in a trap than in a car. Isn't it funny that more people don't drive pony-carts?'

Ann said that she expected it was because cars were easier and quicker, and because the roads were so bad for driving horses in these days. 'And most people even *prefer* cars,' she added.

'How odd,' said Rennie, beginning to enjoy herself enormously, though Shamus was only sedately walking down the lane.

'Oh, I can understand it,' said Ann, pulling a strand of hay out of her jersey. 'You can get quite fond of them,' and she went on to explain how attached Miss Brandon was to her car, though much preferring horses, of course, and how she called it Amelia and talked about its ways as if it were a horse itself. 'In fact, Amelia's a little lame today, and that's one reason why I brought Shamus to meet you. Now, you can trot here, if you like. You just increase the feel on Shamus's mouth a bit – look, like this – you don't have to shake the reins, you know. Properly, we ought to use a whip: not to hit the horse with, of course, but to take the place of legs on a rider. We don't bother with old Shamus, though.'

When she had got used to this new delightful movement – the pony's back bobbing smoothly between the shafts, the harness jingling and creaking and the big wheels humming – Rennie said, 'I thought you were only at the stables in the mornings?'

'I am, really. But when Miss B is specially rushed, I sort of just stay on. She's terribly good, of course, and gives me lunch, and keeps saying, "Are you sure you oughtn't to be getting back?" because I'm supposed to be keeping house for my brother, you know. But I just hate going back until everything's done.'

Rennie looked wistful. 'I do hope I'll be useful,' she said.

'You will be,' said Ann cheerfully, looking at her with the experience of one who has seen stable-girls come and go.

'I seem to have been ill, off and on, for nearly all my life,' said Rennie apologetically. 'Supposing I suddenly flopped, when everyone was at their busiest, and had to go to bed for a week or more? It sometimes happens.'

'You would have to do your own nursing for a bit, I daresay,' Ann said, 'but nobody would *mind*, if that's what you mean. You might even find it doesn't happen here. Nerves are funny things. Now you take the left turning here – but Shamus knows.'

'So do I,' said Rennie. 'That's the field that had the hunters in, and the ponies are in that one.'

'Most of the hunters are in stables now, getting fit for hunting,' said Ann. 'We'll be cubbing next month.'

Rennie suddenly remembered about the make-up. She had been too interested in the driving, and in what Ann was saying, to notice before. She stole a quick glance, not liking to take her eyes off the road, almost as if Shamus had been a car and would run straight into the ditch as soon as she diverted her attention. No, there was no make-up: no doubt at all about it. Ann's nice brown complexion was her own. And her hair was quite ordinary, too. What twists and kinks there were could not be anything but natural, and on anyone else but Ann they might have looked downright untidy. Well, all this wouldn't be very hard to live up to, Rennie thought gratefully, as Shamus drew up in the yard outside the open shed, where an old car that was obviously Amelia stood plainly awaiting her stable companion, Shamus's cart.

No one seemed to be anywhere about, but Ann helped to unload the cases and then backed the trap into its place beside Amelia before beginning to unharness Shamus. 'If you like to take his harness into the tack-room, I'll put him back into the field, and then I'll help you carry your cases to your room,' she said. 'I don't suppose you ought to carry much, just after breaking an arm. You don't mind sharing a room with Sally, do you?'

'No, of course not,' Rennie said, carefully watching the unharnessing process. 'It can't be any worse than a general ward in hospital. The person on one side of me used to grind her teeth in her sleep, and the other one snored.'

Ann laughed. 'You may find that Sally walks! You know where the tack-room is, don't you?'

Rennie nodded, taking Shamus's harness on both arms.

'I won't be long,' Ann said, and led Shamus away by his forelock.

There was no one in the tack-room either, which pleased Rennie, because she was able to have a good look round it by herself after she had put the harness carefully on the bench. It was a fair-sized room, much bigger than Tom Pigram's little shed, and there was a big stove standing right in the middle with its pipe going straight up through the ceiling. Two walls were lined with bridles, each tidily hung up with its throat-lash crossed in front and its owner's name above it on a small white card. There were all kinds of bridles, from little pony-snaffles to full-sized doubles. And all the spaces that were not occupied by bridles or windows or the glass case full of rosettes were lined with racks for saddles, and most of these had saddles on them. So that it looked as if there were not many horses and ponies out this afternoon. Several used bridles hung on a cluster of hanging hooks, no doubt awaiting cleaning, and a pile of rugs lay on a corner chest. Pinned on the wall, near the telephone, was a hand-printed notice, and Rennie went across to read it. It was headed Stable Routine and listed the work to be done every day, with times for doing it, from 'Before breakfast: water, feed, muck out', right through the day, to 'Nine p.m.: water round'. Rennie read it twice over, very carefully, trying to memorize the details, and while she was doing this Ann came swinging round the doorway and said, 'Ready? Oh, are you trying to learn the routine? You'll know it backwards before you've been here a week!'

Rennie said, 'I like the way it gives a time for everything except the early morning work, where it only says "before breakfast"!'

'Oh, well,' said Ann instructively, 'that's because you get up earlier or later according to how many horses have to be done. The work's the same – water, feed, muck out, sweep up the yard; catch up outside horses and ponies; groom; water round again. But it takes longer the more there are.'

'"10 a.m.: Ride or exercise,"' Rennie puzzled. 'What's the difference?'

'If the horses are hired, it's a ride; if they aren't, it's exercise. The stabled ones go out either way.'

'And I suppose "trimming" is tails and manes?'

'And fetlocks – especially with the ponies. They're devils to do, too, because they all live out, and so they're nearly always muddy. The theory is that you should never trim fetlocks when they're wet and muddy, but we often have to, and when they dry out they look just as if someone had trimmed them wet and muddy! Come and look at these photographs of Miss B's in the showcase.'

The photographs were on the opposite wall to the Stable Routine notice, and beside them was another printed notice which said, 'Rides not cancelled the night before – except in cases of sickness or emergency – will be charged for', but the photographs were much more interesting than this.

'This is dear old Hallmark,' Ann was saying. 'Hasn't he got a wonderful head? And he's the kindest horse; Miss B adores him. These are two riding-school groups – this pony's Shamus, and this is Mermaid the skewbald.... Help! is that the ride coming back already? Come on, let's get your cases upstairs.'

# 6 | 'How Lucky I Really Am'

RENNIE felt her way up the wooden stairs to Miss Brandon's front door with her feet, because she was looking over her shoulder all the time at Sally riding in on Mermaid the skewbald, accompanied by three children on ponies and a man on a good-looking brown hunter that she thought was probably Hallmark.

'This is really like a bungalow in mid-air,' Ann was saying. 'Once you're in the house there aren't any more stairs.'

'I think it's lovely – a house with horses downstairs!' Rennie said.

'We could attend to most of the horses without ever going into the open, if the weather were quite awful, by going down through the sitting room trap door.' Ann pushed open Rennie's bedroom door with her knee. 'There you are. I'll dump it by your bed.'

'Can I just put my slacks on and come out and help?'

'Well, I suppose so, but I shouldn't think Miss B expects you to, till the morning.'

Rennie snapped open her biggest case and pulled out the brown corduroys and her heavy lace-up shoes, listening to Ann jumping two at a time down the stairway to the yard. She changed hastily, glancing through a corner window-pane as she did so, but the window only overlooked a little lawn with roses round it and the lane leading out to the village, and the only sign of life was the Cairn, Puffin, walking slowly up the lane as a change from family life.

It would have been fun to go down through the trap-door, but when you were new you didn't do things like that, so Rennie flew back down the outdoor stairway again, and continued more cautiously round the corner and into the yard. She had never worn slacks before, and felt like somebody quite different, which was a nice sort of feeling, because she didn't want to feel like her old self at all. The slacks and jersey suited her really well, because of her boyish figure and hairstyle, and they were comfortable and workmanlike as well.

In the yard the brown hunter and one of the innumerable small bay ponies stood tied to the wall, and Sally was brushing wet mud from their hoofs with a dandy-brush and a bucket of water. The man who had been riding stood talking to her as she worked, but the other people seemed to have gone. Rennie hesitated. 'Yes, it's me! What shall I do?'

'Well, perhaps you could put Hallmark in his box for me, and see if his water needs filling up. It's the first one on the left, next to the feed-room. You'd never think there'd be all this mud about, would you? but we went through the Blue Ride, and it's always pretty moist down there. Oh, by the way, this is Maurice – Maurice Lowe. He rides with us. Maurice, this is Rennie Jordan, our new helper.'

Rennie said how-do-you-do and untied Hallmark's halter-rope from a ring in the wall. The old horse clattered placidly down the covered passage between the loose-boxes, with his head by Rennie's shoulder. She led him into his box, saw that his water-bucket was full, then unbuckled his bridle and took it to the tack-room, where Ann had made a start on cleaning saddles. A bucket of hot water steamed gently on the floor and a large white kitten sat cosily up against it. Ann said, 'Would you rather do saddles or bridles?'

'I can't say until I find out!'

'Most people prefer saddles: they haven't so many fiddly bits.

Shall I show you? It's awfully easy really. First you clean them with a damp rag, like this, to get off all the grease and mud, starting on the inside. You needn't undo the buckles except on hunting days: there simply isn't time for Rotten Row standards here. Then you go all over the leather with a saddle-soap sponge. You can't use too much saddle-soap, and you must rub it well in, but you have to keep your sponge wrung out so that you don't start getting a lather. Now, here's a cleaning-rag, and a soap-sponge, and here's the soap. You can start on Cobweb's saddle, as it's a nice small one.'

There was a sudden light rush and the white kitten was on Rennie's shoulders.

'Snowy always does that,' Ann said. 'Sally taught her; she's her kitten. Miss B only let her keep it because we all thought it was a he. Now we think it's a she, but it's a bit late for Miss B to change her mind, at four months. Anyway, tip her off if you don't want her.'

'I like her,' Rennie said, rubbing Cobweb's saddle.

Sally put her head round the door. 'I'll come and help when I've put Cobweb back. Maurice is coming again on Wednesday, and the two Lister children tomorrow.'

'Right,' said Ann, and went to jot it down in a notebook by the telephone. Cobweb's hoofs clattered through the yard and then suddenly went muffled on the track outside.

'Maurice is the one who was riding Hallmark,' Ann said, coming back to the saddle-horse and dipping her sponge.

'I know. I met him.'

'He used to be one of the best riders in Hampshire.'

'Isn't he still?'

'Haven't you ever heard of Maurice Lowe?'

Rennie wrinkled her brow. 'I don't think so. Ought I to have?'

'Well, he was in the papers and all that, after his hunting accident. He was in hospital for quite a time, but the really odd thing was his forgetting all about riding.'

Rennie lifted the saddle-flaps to clean underneath them. 'About the accident, you mean?'

'No, about riding altogether – everything he ever knew about it, practically. But he remembered everything else. In fact, except for that one kink he's exactly the same as before.'

'It doesn't seem possible,' Rennie said.

'The longer I live, the more I come to realize that anything's possible,' said Ann wisely. 'Now where did I put my soap-sponge? Oh, here. Well, what Maurice is doing now is learning to ride again, right from the beginning. And we're teaching him. Those Lister children are his niece and nephew, and he often comes with them. It's a good idea, because we can get a lot of teaching through to him by teaching them. It does save him some of the embarrassment. Well, think of teaching someone how to canter who's won cups for jumping and racing.'

'Does he know he did?' Rennie's shoulders swung as she rubbed, and Snowy rode them like a sailor on a shifting deck.

'Of course. There are all his cups and things to prove it. But he knows he's forgotten, too. He's very sensible about it.'

Rennie said doubtfully. 'You wouldn't think he'd want to come here to learn. I mean, you'd think he'd rather be taught by a man.'

'Miss B has a terribly good reputation,' Ann said. 'And besides, John and Janet Lister had already been coming for some time, and he often brought them. But the real reason, I think,' she added, 'is Sally. If it hadn't been for his accident, I think they might have become engaged. So far as I know, he hasn't said anything to Sally about it since, but Sally only tells you what she wants you to know. I do know she still thinks a lot of him, though.'

'Poor Sally,' Rennie said; 'it must be awful; and I hope it never happens to me. But in any case, I'm much too young at present.'

'And you look younger. But Sally's only eighteen, you know. How old d'you think I am?' she suddenly asked, grinning.

Rennie looked at her over the saddles and said, 'I'm no good at all at guessing ages. Miss Brandon said you were much older than Sally, so that must put you at quite twenty, I suppose.'

Ann laughed, taking her saddle to put it away on its bracket. 'I'm nearer thirty than twenty. Sometimes I feel awfully old. To begin with, I've retired! I ran my own riding-school for seven years before I decided to give up and keep house for Robert. But here I am, at it again.'

'Like Tom Pigram,' Rennie said. 'He reckons he's busier now he's retired. You must know an awful lot about horses,' she added wistfully. 'Miss Brandon said you were very experienced and reliable, but if I'd known you'd had your own place for all those years, I'd never have dared to come at all. I was terrified enough, as it was. For one thing, I thought you would be extremely smart.'

'You should see me on hunting days!' said Ann. 'All the same,' she added seriously, 'I always *intend* to look tidier and smarter. I mean, I do put lipstick on, and that sort of thing, when I think about it. The trouble is, so often I don't think about it. Five o'clock in the morning is no sort of time for titivation, and all too often there never seems to be a moment later on. Or if there is, I forget it. Sally's better, but then she has more reason.'

'Did somebody say something about me?' Sally inquired, coming round the door.

'I said that you were tidier than I am.'

'I hope I am!' said Sally.

And then Miss Brandon was in the doorway.

'I'm sorry I was busy when you came, Rennie; but you seem to have settled in very nicely by yourself. How would you like to come and help me do the boxes and water, as Sally's in to help with the tack, now?'

'Oh, yes!' said Rennie. 'I've just finished this saddle.'

'It goes on the bracket by the window,' Ann said, and Rennie lifted it up, causing Snowy to slither down her back to the floor again.

There was a convenient tap at the near end of the main stables passage, where Rennie filled the two spare buckets, carrying them up the lines of boxes to top up the horses' own buckets. Only Hallmark could put his head out into the passage, all the other boxes having barred windows and high doors, but he watched all that went on, as was fitting in the Grand Old Man of the stables. At first Rennie half expected to be nipped as she passed almost under his nose along the narrow way, but he only blew at her inquiringly. Barbemusche, the tall chestnut, frightened her badly by snaking his head at her as she went in with his water, laying his ears flat and showing the whites of his eyes.

'I don't think he really means anything,' Miss Brandon said reassuringly, coming in with a bucket and dung-fork to tidy his bed; 'but he isn't a very friendly horse in his box. Out in the field he's hardly the same horse: follows me about, trotting beside me, as nicely as you could wish. If only he knew what a difference it makes when he puts his ears forward!' she added, holding them forward for a minute for Rennie to see, before giving him an affectionate slap and reaching for her tools again.

Rennie tried not to catch his eye as she filled up his water-bucket, because of letting him see how scared she was, and went thankfully on to Brown Jane in the next box.

There was no time for a proper break for tea, because of further bookings in the evening ('We can usually count on extra bookings for fine summer evenings,' Miss Brandon said), but Sally brought down a tray of 'tack-room tea' after Ann had belatedly bicycled home, and the saddles and bridles were finished while cake and tea were being consumed. The telephone rang twice during this informal meal; once to cancel a ride because of toothache and an emergency visit to the dentist, and once for a booking in the morning. And directly the last crumb had been eaten, and the last bridle hung up again, the horses for the evening ride had to be got ready.

'Brown Jane, Julia, and Flossie,' Miss Brandon was saying; 'for our three elderly ladies, Rennie,' she explained. 'The Misses Frogley, Fenney, and Eade.'

Sally gave a sudden snort of laughter, and Miss Brandon looked at her reproachfully. 'You and Ann always laugh at my old ladies, but I think they're really rather nice old things,' she said.

'You'd think, when they've been riding for fifteen years, that they'd have learnt *some*thing about it, by now,' said Sally, reaching for Julia's saddle.

'Oh, I don't know,' said Miss Brandon tolerantly. 'At least they do leave their horses' mouths alone.'

'That's half the trouble,' said Sally. 'They haven't any contact.'

'It's better than too much, I do assure you,' said Miss Brandon, 'and I speak from the bottom of a well of experience with heavy-handed riders. Rennie, here's Flossie's bridle. How about having a go at putting it on, while I saddle her? And Sally, don't forget a saddle-pad for Julia.'

With a little preliminary instruction and a demonstration, Rennie didn't do at all badly in bridling Flossie, but Miss Brandon loosened the throat-lash by a couple of holes and tightened the nose-band.

'Now, what are we going to put you on?'

'Am I coming, too?' Rennie's face suddenly lightened.

'Well, it seems a good opportunity. The Three Graces never ride fast or far, and it's a lovely evening. How about Spindle? He really is just about a perfect pony for an older beginner. Ask Sally if she can fetch him up for you, while you change into your jodhpurs.'

Spindle certainly was a perfect pony, as far as Rennie was concerned. He was a good-looking bright bay of nearly fifteen hands, with mane and tail, and he radiated such a feeling of quiet confidence that Rennie's nervousness sank down at once into the lower layers of her mind. Unlike the young Templar, he was wise and experienced in this riding business, and knew exactly what was expected of him. Rennie felt that, if she should make some awful mistake herself, Spindle would understand and make his own sensible adjustments so that everything would come right in the end. He was so quiet for handling and saddling and bridling that Rennie half expected him to be a 'slug' when out riding, and that she would get left farther and farther behind because of her inability to 'ride him on'. But Spindle's perfections included nearly all things, except, Miss Brandon told Rennie, show conformation and absolute reliability about nipping. With Rennie on his back, and elderly ladies all around him, he walked on gaily with a smooth, free stride; and suddenly Rennie realized that, for the first time in the whole of her life, she was doing the one thing she had always wanted to do, and that it was as glorious as she had ever imagined.

Riding Spindle was so entirely unlike riding Templar that Rennie hardly felt she could be doing the same sort of thing at all. Even though she had no experience and very little knowledge in the matter, she was able to enjoy riding Spindle as she had never enjoyed anything else before, as far as she could remember. Miss Brandon showed her how to hold the reins correctly, and explained about knee-grip and keeping heels and elbows down, but Rennie had read all these things many times for herself, and now only required to learn how to do them without continuous concentration and effort. At the walk things were fairly easy, and she found that she could spare quite a lot of her mind for enjoying the heavenly August evening, with robins singing their thin, autumn-sounding song in the high hedges, and mackerel clouds like feathers over the wide Hampshire hills.

She enjoyed the old ladies very much, too, and decided that she agreed both with Sally that they were comical and with

Miss Brandon that they were really rather nice. And surely they must be very sporting, too, considering that they all appeared to be well into their sixties; so that even if they had been riding ineffectually for fifteen years as Sally said, they must have been nearing fifty when they first began – an age when many women believe in taking life slowly and comfortably.

Miss Brandon was charming with them, when one considered what a trouble they were to her. Every few minutes, it seemed, one of them would need some little assistance, or reassurance, or praise from her, as if they had been quite young children. It was 'Jean, Jean! I think my saddle's slipping' and 'Oh, Jean! are you sure my stirrups are the same length they usually are? They do feel funny' and 'Jean! *did* you see? I jumped that little tree-trunk by the path.'

It was when they all started trotting that Rennie's real troubles began, because she found it so difficult to learn to 'rise' properly, and bumped poor Spindle's saddle in a most breathless way: and then suddenly she discovered how to do it, as one suddenly discovers how to ride a bicycle. For a moment she felt almost like little Miss Eade, and called out, 'Miss Brandon! Look! I'm rising to the trot.'

Miss Brandon was very pleased about this. 'Some people bounce at the trot for days and days,' she said. 'But of course Spindle has a very smooth action. You're lucky to be learning on him.'

'I'm lucky altogether,' said Rennie seriously. 'I don't think anybody but me could know how lucky I really am.'

'Oh, Jean!' said Miss Fenny earnestly, 'do you think you could look at Jane's shoes? I think one of them is coming loose.'

# 7 Morning Ride

RENNIE's wonderful hour on Spindle became only the first of very many; and because of this, and because of Spindle's sweet reliability, he became her favourite horse of all of them.

'Not more favourite than Hallmark?' Sally asked one morning in September when they were leading in ponies from the near field. 'I don't see how anyone can like any horse better than Hall. He has so much character, and such a nice character, too. I mean, think how fond and fatherly he is with all the other horses and ponies.'

Rennie was leading the little bay Jenny Wren, and the moorland pony Cobweb; their backs and manes wet and steamy from a sudden autumn shower. 'But Spindle taught me to ride,' she said, 'as well as to be more confident with horses. And I wouldn't have been much use to Hallmark or any of the others without that. I think I shall still remember Spindle gratefully when I'm a very old woman. He never once took advantage of me, even on that awful day when I forgot to tighten up his girths and the saddle slipped.'

Sally was sitting astride black Shamus and leading Gingersnap and Pixie, in the capable way that Rennie envied but had not yet the confidence to try herself. 'Well, you're graduating this morning. I hear you're riding Mermaid.'

'Yes. It's exciting in a way I suppose, but I know I shall miss Spindle.'

Sally said, 'We're promoting Maurice this morning, too. He's going to ride Barbemusche. John and Janet can have Cobweb and Jenny Wren, and Ann's riding the Stranger.'

'Aren't you coming, then?'

'No,' said Sally shortly, and jerked Gingersnap's head because he snatched at a tuft of roadside grass. 'I've got to take the kids' class this afternoon instead, because Miss B is going to have her hair done, and Ann won't be here.'

'And I'm as good as not here, when it comes to anything really useful,' said Rennie wistfully. Then, as an afterthought as they turned up to the stables, 'Couldn't I do whatever you're doing this morning, so that you could go out on both rides? I really wouldn't mind. I've had much more than a ride a day, lately.'

'Thanks,' said Sally, 'but I'm afraid you wouldn't be much good at that, either. I've got to pull manes and tails ready for cubbing tomorrow. Jester's and Julia's are absolute thickets, and Jester is wicked to do unless we put a twitch on him. Then I've got three to take to the forge.'

Rennie said nothing, feeling too cast down about her uselessness to be able to think of anything, but Sally added a last remark as she jumped down from Shamus that was almost double-edged, and odd from her: 'Anyway, I don't suppose Maurice will mind, since he gets on so well with you now. I daresay he thinks you have a lot in common, being another psychological case, so to speak.'

Rennie pondered uneasily about this as she took Jenny Wren and Cobweb to the pony-boxes, and then she forgot about it in the rush of cleaning their muddy coats and the excitement of saddling up Mermaid for herself. Mermaid was such a nice, lightweight little cob, and the bold patches of her skewbald coat had a gay air that was emphasized by her swinging walk.

John and Janet Lister came running down the passage between the loose-boxes when Rennie was buckling Mermaid's bridle.

'We've come! May we saddle and bridle our own ponies,

please? We couldn't find Ann to ask her,' said John.

'Are you really riding Mermaid?' Janet asked.

'Yes, isn't it exciting? She's ready now, so I can help you saddle the ponies.'

'Uncle Maurice was looking for Sally,' Janet said; and Rennie thought thank goodness for that, and then she thought how really awful it must be to be in love.

'May we look at Puffin's puppies? Is Snowy in the feed-room?' asked John, walking down the passage with a jumping step.

'After the ride. See if you can find your bridles while I reach the saddles down.'

Suddenly Ann tore into the tack-room, reaching for Dark Stranger's bridle all in one movement. 'Everything happens at once. First I ripped the seam in my jodhs on the door-key and had to mend it; and then the sink went and blocked up on Mrs Waddy and I had that awful job of poking slimy dish-mop ends out of the U-bend with one of her hairpins; and then, out of gratefulness, she wanted to show me the photographs of all her grandchildren, and I hadn't the heart to say no. Weak-minded, that's me.' And she rushed out again with her saddle and bridle.

Miss Brandon was striding about with side-saddles, getting Brown Jane and Julia and Flossie ready for the three old ladies, and saying that they really ought to have another horse; and Maurice and Sally were saddling Barbemusche in his box, and Puffin was waddling about in a slightly distracted manner, wanting to forget her children for a while but not being very good at it. And then, when Rennie had seen John and Janet properly mounted and was hurrying back to see if Ann and Maurice were ready and to bring out Mermaid, the three old ladies suddenly arrived in a pre-war Ford which they were very fond of and had christened Old Velocity. The stables, which had seemed full enough before, now seemed to bulge with people and horses and ponies and cats and dogs – because, though Puffin was only one small dog, she had a remarkable capacity for being in four places at once.

Then Mandy arrived. Rennie was very fond of Mandy, who spent a lot of her evenings and week-ends and holidays at Kingwood Stables. She was a sensible, quiet eleven-year-old who kept her own pony, Acorn, with Miss Brandon, though she really shared Rennie's preference for Spindle. 'And he never nips me,' she once said to Rennie, 'because he knows he's my favourite horse.'

'May I come with you and Ann?' she asked when Rennie was leading Mermaid through the crowded yard. And then in a whisper, 'I don't really want to go with the Three Graces, and it isn't half such fun alone.'

'You'll have to be awfully quick, then, Mandy; we're just starting.'

'Oh, I will,' said Mandy confidently. 'I can take my bridle and catch Acorn in the field and be on the road almost before you. I needn't bother about a saddle, for once. And anyway, Miss B says it's good practice and everyone ought to ride without a saddle sometimes.'

'But not muddy, my girl! not from these stables,' said Ann, coming down the passage with the Edwardian-looking Dark Stranger.

'I can take a dandy-brush and leave it by the gate-post,' said Mandy resourcefully. 'Then I'll catch you up.' In four seconds she was gone, the bridle and dandy in her hands, dashing round the buildings to the field where Acorn was grazing.

Rennie mounted Mermaid from the stone block outside the yard, while Sally held Barbemusche for Maurice, and Ann pulled up the children's girths with the Stranger's rein round one arm. The voices of the Three Graces drifted out to them from the stables: 'Jean! I've put on Flossie's bridle; do come and see if it's all right. It's the curb-chain that really bothers me.' And, 'Oh, Jean! I think there's a bit of hay under Jane's saddle. Had we better get it out?'

'Everyone ready?' said Ann, settling her reins and looking round at her party. 'Squeeze Cobweb with your legs, Janet. That's the idea. Don't pull too tightly on the reins, or he'll think you want him to stay still. All right, Maurice?'

They were moving off now, through a thinning mist and as they rounded the tall cherry laurels on the corner Rennie could see Mandy in the Park field feverishly brushing down Acorn, with a close-pressing audience of other ponies who had seen the apple-bits that Acorn had been beguiled with.

'Barbemusche isn't really a bad ride at all,' Ann was saying to Maurice, who was riding beside her. 'It's only in the stable that he's so very disagreeable.'

'But I think he just puts it on, don't you?' Maurice said; and Rennie, riding behind them with the ponies, found it hard to believe in his old riding prowess, as she always did. He didn't look much more secure on Barbemusche than she felt on Mermaid, but he was quicker to learn than anyone else who came to the stables.

'It's quite an honour, really,' Ann said to Maurice, 'Miss B giving you Barbemusche. She's rather touchy about him, you know – thinks people will ruin his mouth and all that; but he certainly does only go his best for people with the sort of light hands that still maintain contact.'

Mandy caught them up at a fast trot near the railway bridge, and Rennie fell back to ride with her, listening sympathetically as she talked about not having a single dog.

'Even one of Puffin's puppies would be lovely to have, but what I really want is a dog from Battersea Dogs' Home, or a place like that. You know, one that would never have had a happy home. But mother doesn't like dogs' – she sighed a little – 'and whenever I mention it she just says that Acorn is really enough expense.'

Rennie said, 'You can always play with Puffin's puppies at the stables.'

Mandy pressed Acorn on with her heels to keep up with

Mermaid's long stride. 'I know. But they have a happy home already. If I ever get married,' she added seriously, 'I don't think I shall have any children of my own. I shall adopt them all from an Institution.'

Rennie thought about this and then came to the conclusion that she rather agreed. 'And especially,' she said, 'if one could give them a really good country life, such as on a farm, or a house in a village where they could keep ponies.'

'And dogs,' said Mandy eagerly, making Acorn walk faster; 'don't forget dogs, Rennie; they go with horses so well, don't you think?'

Ann loved teaching, as she had several times told Rennie. She was sure that she did it well, and had decided that she had a vocation for it. She had been teaching Maurice as the party clattered round the twisty lane, but when they came up on to the open common she drew rein and waited for the ponies.

'Now, how about some exercises, John and Janet? You can join in too, if you like, Mandy, but it's old stuff for you.'

The Lister children squared their shoulders and settled themselves in their saddles, looking expectantly at Ann.

'Now, keep quietly walking on.... Swing one arm as if you were cowboys swinging their lassos. That's the way! Now take your feet out of the stirrups ... Turn your toes up ... and then down. Now, turn right round and look at your ponies' tails. Now the other way ... and back the other way ...'

Rennie found herself riding with Maurice, a little ahead of Ann and the three ponies.

'She really enjoys herself,' said Maurice, in friendly amusement.

'She likes teaching,' Rennie said, picking Mermaid's way round the boggy places.

'It must be nice to know just what you want to do, and like doing it,' said Maurice.

'It is,' Rennie said. 'I've always known what I wanted to do, and now I'm doing it I'm enjoying myself enormously.'

'I expect you have a lot of courage,' Maurice said, 'and that makes a difference. Now I'm scared to death of horses – honestly. Especially in the stable.'

Rennie glanced at him disbelievingly. He looked what he was – a successful young working farmer; but he didn't look afraid.

'It's only because of your accident, I expect,' she said; and then, because someone else could openly and cheerfully admit to a thing that she herself had concealed as a disgraceful secret, she added firmly, 'I'm terrified of horses, myself. But don't mention it, in case I lose my job! All the same, I think working with them is the finest thing to do in the world.'

# 8 | Sleepless Night, and Initiating Robin

RENNIE was alone in the yard a little later when the first real test of her courage suddenly happened. They had just come in from the ride and she had helped John and Janet to unsaddle their ponies and take them back to the field, while Maurice and Sally scrubbed the muddy hoofs of Dark Stranger and Barbemusche and took them to their boxes. Mermaid was waiting, tied to one of the wall-rings, and Rennie got to work with a fresh bucket of water and a dandy-brush, taking care not to let the water splash up on to Mermaid's pasterns. A wasp had been buzzing around them, but Rennie never minded wasps and took no notice. Perhaps the wasp got itself entangled in Mermaid's mane; no one quite knew; but all at once she was rearing madly, pawing the air and the wall and just missing Rennie's bent head with her slashing hoofs. Rennie ducked quickly out of range as Mermaid came down; and then she saw with horrified eyes that one of the mare's forelegs was caught up over the halter-rope.

Rennie stood for a moment gripped with fear and indecision. Oh, what to do? Panic crashed around inside her chest. The rope was drawn so tightly that it dragged down Mermaid's head. Rennie tugged desperately at the slip-knot, but it had pulled too tightly to slip. She grasped the hooked-up leg and tried to lift it free, but Mermaid could do nothing while her head was held down low. The mare began to tremble, as if she might fall to the ground, and then suddenly Ann was there –

Ann, who always knew what to do – and she had sliced through the rope with one quick slash with the knife that she always carried. Mermaid threw up her head sharply, and then drew a deep shuddery breath.

'Good thing my knife was sharp,' said Ann calmly. 'What happened?'

Rennie told her briefly, her old stutter coming back. She was patting and stroking the little skewbald to reassure her.

'Good thing Miss B isn't back. She always worries,' said Ann. 'Now finish her hoofs and take her back to her box. Then we must fly round the water-buckets and boxes before the Graces come back, or Mrs Waddy'll be complaining again that we always spoil her cooking by keeping it waiting. And there's chaff to cut as well.'

For a dreadful few moments Rennie thought that her hands were going limp. Then she was suddenly sure that she was going at the knees. Ann had dashed off again to make a start on tidying boxes, and Sally was somewhere up the passage rolling tail-bandages. Maurice and the Lister children had gone, and Mandy was watering in the pony-stables. No one saw Rennie's panicky battle with herself; not even Mermaid, who was too preoccupied with all that had just happened to her. Rennie put out a hand and leaned against the wall. Snowy, the white kitten, came lightly trotting out of the tack-room and ran up on to her shoulders, purring. Then Rennie took a grip on herself, made up her mind that her knees and hands were going to do just what she wanted of them, and she grasped hold of the cut end of Mermaid's halter-rope.

Sally glanced up from her bandage-rolling as Rennie passed her with Mermaid, the kitten still riding on her shoulder.

'You had a bit of a shemozzle down there?' she said inquiringly, pressing herself to the wall to let them pass.

Rennie nodded, leading Mermaid into her end box.

'You should have seen Ann once, when she was holding Jester to have a torn eye-lid dressed, and he reared up and struck her face. Her cheek-bone was cracked; have you ever noticed the little dent there?'

'I d-don't think so.' Rennie was putting Mermaid's rug on; remembering, in spite of her shock, to throw it on well up the neck and then draw it smoothly backwards so that every hair lay flat and comfortable. Somewhere inside her a small feeling of elation began to push up through the shaky feeling of subsiding panic – elation because she was almost sure that, this time, her nerves were not going to get the better of her. Then, possibly, she really was already improving? though she had only been at Kingwood for a fortnight, the high hope of one day being as well as Ann or Sally suddenly strengthened.

But a life of nervous illness was not as easily overcome as that, it seemed, for that night Rennie had a return of fearful nightmares. Three times she woke both Sally and Miss Brandon with horrified screaming, and the horror was not for Mermaid but for her own mother trapped under the car. After the second time Sally felt a little impatient. There was the cubbing meet in the morning, and that meant a four o'clock start to their day, for cubbing horses always left before dawn, and must be fed and groomed a good hour beforehand. But Miss Brandon had deep wells of patience, born of long years of solitary responsibility, of coping with difficult horses, awkward clients, and severe money losses due to long runs of bad weather. She sat between Rennie's and Sally's beds, wrapped closely in a camel dressing-gown, and radiated calm serenity until, feeling rather like a sick horse that Miss Brandon was faithfully watching over, Rennie went to sleep; but only to wake again screaming, with that dreadful noise of car-brakes in her ears.

Everyone felt a little worn the next morning – excepting Ann, of course, who, having slept soundly, turned up at five on her bicycle as briskly cheerful and efficient as usual. Miss Brandon had not allowed Rennie to be woken early, so that when she did wake up, seeing the time by her watch and dressing quickly in a panic, the early work was already done and the cubbing horses long since gone. A note from Miss Brandon was left pinned on the kitchen-door where Rennie would see it.

'No stable work for you till after breakfast: but you can get breakfast on if you like. Miss B.'

Rennie did like. Throwing up the window to the morning sunshine, she whirled around with knives and spoons and plates, dodging the ginger tom and a very shiny black cat called Bosky and Snowy's white mother.

Leading out from the kitchen was the comfortable living-room, where meals were always eaten at the stable flat. Anyone would have known that it was the room of a horsy household, because wherever one looked there were horse calendars and pictures on the walls, and a fox's brush by the door, with a coaching-horn over the lintel. The big sideboard was crowded with photographs of horses, past and present, and several horsy papers lay scattered on the window-sill. There were three deep, comfortable chairs, a wood-burning stove and a big round table on which Rennie was now setting the breakfast-things.

She made a panful of porridge on the gas-stove, carefully following the directions on the packet, and covered it to keep it warm; and she was just lifting down the frying-pan from its shelf when Ann and Sally and Miss Brandon came stamping up the wooden stairs from the stables.

'This is wonderful,' said Miss Brandon. 'I quite expected you would still be asleep, as you had so little last night.'

'You and Sally had much less.' Rennie felt ashamed of her extra hours, when Sally and Miss Brandon had been working hard since long before dawn.

'It reminds me,' said Ann cheerfully, washing her hands at the sink, 'of the old villager who asked the chemist for some aspirins – "the biggest box you've got; I wouldn't ever get a good night's sleep without they." "You mustn't take too many at once; they're dangerous, you know," the chemist told him, a bit shocked; but the old chap said, "Oh, I never take any at all. I give them to my old woman." '

Everybody laughed, and Rennie forgot about the bacon and frizzled it, and then it turned out that everybody except herself liked it frizzled. Ann noticed in her practical way that the kettle was not on and remedied the matter; and Sally fed the cats; so that breakfast was not much later than usual, despite the cubbing and the short-handedness. It was nearly finished when Mrs Waddy was heard puffing and blowing as she mounted the outside stairway.

'I brought you a nice bit of stewing steak, dear,' she said to Miss Brandon from the little lobby where she was hanging her coat. 'Now if I start that early, on a slow gas, it'll make a lovely stew with barley and dumplings, what won't spoil if you're in late, as is more'n likely.'

The postman came as everyone was pulling on jackets again, and the letters were taken down to the tack-room so that Mrs Waddy could have a clear house.

Sitting on the corner bench, Rennie tore open a letter from Robin. Hearing of his sustained interest in the ponies, Miss Brandon had said with her usual acute understanding: 'Perhaps he would like to come and help with them a bit, sometimes, and have a ride or two in exchange. Would he be any good at cleaning tack, d'you think?' And this was Robin's answer to Rennie's letter:

'Dear Rennie,

'Whacko! I'm coming tomorrow – today when you get this – what a pity school starts next week.

Love, Robin.'

Miss Brandon smiled when Rennie showed it to her. 'What a shame about school! We could have asked him before, but I thought you would rather not have him around when you were first learning. Oh, well, let me see; Cobweb's really the best pony for a small beginner; Robin could have him this morning, as we've only got Finner and Fatter besides the cubbing people, and they'll want Shamus and Snowcloud as usual, I expect.'

'Two friends, both called Jennifer,' Ann explained to Rennie. 'When they first came here, and were very small, Finner couldn't pronounce her own name and called herself Jennifinner. She always was the thinner of the two, and it was useful to have some way of distinguishing them, so they became Finner and Fatter. They're about ten years old now, and jolly good little riders, except that Fatter is downright reckless if you don't keep an eye on her.'

Miss Brandon said, turning back to her own letter, 'I do believe I've found a horse.'

Ann had just lifted down Hallmark's saddle and stared at her over it. 'But Miss B, you've got too many already! What you really need is to start cutting down somewhere, not buying in. Doesn't she, Sally?'

Sally said, 'Cutting down where, then?'

'That's just it,' said Miss Brandon. 'I know we do seem to have an awful lot of horses and ponies, but the thing is, where to begin? I can't really cut down anywhere, as far as I can see; except, perhaps, with the ponies. But we need them all when Kingwood School starts, and the boys' riding classes have to be arranged.'

'I'm sure it doesn't pay,' said Ann. 'The thing you ought to remember, dear Miss B, is the winter. Frost and snow, and cancelled rides. No money coming in and all the horses still to feed and the rent to pay.'

Miss Brandon sighed reminiscently, a distant look on her face, but Sally said encouragingly, 'What sort of horse have you heard of, now?'

'He's a big heavy-weight cob called Sir Richard. Up to a lot of weight, and goes well to hounds. I used to know his owner pretty well, so I think he'll be genuine enough, and the price is reasonable. The point is, we haven't really got anything now that's fit to carry a really heavy rider, like Major Cornelius, and you can't always get what you want at a price you can pay. One has to consider one's best clients. Brown Jane isn't really up to the Major's weight. You haven't met him yet,' she added to Rennie, 'but you will when the hunting starts.'

'But you can't buy a horse just for one client,' said Ann reasonably, adding Hallmark's saddle-pad, martingale, and bridle to the saddle on her arm.

'Well, we shall just have to canvas round for some more heavy clients!' said Sally.

'The vicar, the grocer's wife, and old Mr Cheadle at Pond Farm,' said Miss Brandon, amusing herself by thinking of a few. 'Oh well, this won't butter any parsnips.... How about riding Mermaid again today, Rennie?'

'I thought she was out cubbing?'

'No. I changed my mind at the last minute and sent Jester instead. She seemed to be starting a lump on her head, when we were doing stables early this morning. I don't know what it is, but I don't expect a gentle hack will hurt her.'

'Didn't anyone tell you about yesterday – when she got her leg over the halter-rope?'

Miss Brandon looked from Ann to Sally, and back at Rennie inquiringly. So Rennie told her, while the other two went off to begin saddling up.

'Well, I can't see that any of it was your fault,' said Miss Brandon fairly. 'Anyway, thank you for telling me: we do at least know what caused the bump, now. I expect there was a lot of pressure from the halter, over her head; but probably the lump will go down in a day or two. I'll tell you one thing we will do from today, though. We'll have string loops on all the tying-rings, and tie the horses up to those, so that if any more trouble happens the string will break. That way, we ought to eliminate broken bridles and halters as well as hurt horses.'

When Rennie was out fetching up Cobweb for Robin she saw him bicycling madly down the hill and waving as he did so.

'This is Cobweb,' she told him when she had brought the pony to the gate. 'You're riding him this morning!'

'What? Before working for it? Oh, I say!'

'You can work as hard as you like afterwards!' Rennie grinned. 'I'll wheel your bicycle if you'd like to lead him.'

The pure pleasure of taking her small brother for his very first ride was chilled for Rennie that morning, because all the way she could quite easily see the bump just behind Mermaid's ears, and she was certain that if anyone except herself had been in charge at that awful moment it wouldn't have happened. But one thing she decided was to save up for a really good clasp-knife and carry it with her everywhere.

Finner and Fatter were so full of vigour and dash that it became quite exhausting watching them. They jumped every fallen tree two or three times over, they opened all the gates for Sally and Rennie and Robin, practised circling on the right hand and the left hand, and bending among the trees in Farthing Wood. They bemoaned the end of the gymkhana season and the approach of school, and said they wished they were out with the cub-hunters.

Robin was awed into blissful quietness as he rode the wise old Cobweb at Rennie's side, but he watched the reckless progress of Finner and Fatter with the sort of absorbed expression that meant he knew that he would one day be doing the same himself, incredible though it might seem now.

Sally seemed to have got over her moment of bitterness about Maurice, and she bore no grudge for her broken night, so that she was able to fill up other people's silences with cheerful talk of horses, clients, and hunting.

Mermaid's bump looked just as big – or bigger, Rennie felt sure – by the time they got back; but as the cubbing horses had come in just before them, there was so much work to do that no one had much time to worry about it. Five sets of muddy hoofs had first to be scrubbed clean, but Rennie noticed string loops fitted already to the tying-rings, and so was able to help at this job without pangs of acute apprehension. Finner and Fatter were perfectly capable of seeing to their own ponies, and did so with great efficiency. They also decided to make themselves responsible for initiating Robin into stable life, and carefully explained to him all that was to be done for Cobweb while they set the example with Shamus and Snowcloud. After this they stayed on to help with watering and feeding, so that Rennie and Sally were able to get a mound of chaff cut while Ann and Miss Brandon worked at cleaning muddy horses in their boxes.

'We'll be late for lunch again,' said Sally, turning the big chaff-cutter wheel as Rennie pushed the hay towards the cogs. 'Poor Mrs. Waddy! the things she suffers from us.'

Presently Sally had stopped to rest, clutching her back and puffing breathlessly. 'I'm always sure I've got lumbago, whenever I wind that awful wheel.'

They changed places for a while, and then Rennie was puffing and clasping her back, peeling her pullover off, and starting again. Then Sally began sneezing because of the hay-dust, and when Miss Brandon came in to measure out feeds they both looked as though their hours were numbered. But Miss Brandon was used to the evil ways of the chaff-cutter and took no notice, only peering short-sightedly into the feed-bins and saying a little absently: 'Bran's getting a bit low, and it isn't due till Friday. Perhaps I could bring a sack back in Amelia this afternoon. She's such a good-hearted car, she won't take exception if it leaks inside her.'

# 9 | Veterinary Report

ROBIN proved to be most useful when he could be kept going at a job. But he was young enough to be continually side-tracked by all the cats and Puffin and her puppies, wanting everyone else to come and look at them as well, but not getting much response from a busy staff. He had brought a sandwich lunch and tea, so that he was no trouble, and he stayed until about an hour before sunset, which enabled him to get through an amazing amount of useful little jobs, despite the fascination of the animals.

Mandy came in the afternoon, and she and Robin cleaned so much tack – and fairly well – that the pile of saddles and bridles from the cub-hunters was considerably reduced by the time Tom Pigram arrived to help with them, just before tea.

'Looks like someone been doing me out of a job,' he said, stilting into the tack-room on his stick-legs with his long jaw poked out inquiringly. 'Well, so long as they done 'em thorough.' He directed a searching look at Robin and Mandy, who were cheerfully cleaning saddles under the window and eating the remains of their shared sandwiches at the same time.

The evening sun slanted in through the dusty windows and twinkled on bits and buckles and stirrup-irons. The bucket of hot water steamed gently by the unlit stove, and Snowy sat leaning against it as usual in a blissful dream of warmth. The tack-room smelt pleasantly of leather and saddle-soap and horses. It was full of the comfortable sounds of jingling and rubbing and talking and purring, and it was littered with the gloves and whips and jackets and mackintoshes that people had just put down while cleaning the tack, and with the rugs and saddle-pads that somehow hadn't been put in the chest. There was a large dilapidated armchair that anybody could collapse in if in the last stages of exhaustion – it usually held Puffin and two cats – a couple of old Windsor chairs and a long bench with its three drawers full of tack-cleaning materials, first-aid equipment, and general stable oddments such as scissors and clippers and spare tail-bandages.

'Miss B's back,' said Sally, coming in with a loaded tray. 'It's tack-room tea again, so that we can finish early for once.'

Rennie followed her in with the kettle and tea-pot, but Miss Brandon went down through the stables to look at Mermaid before she joined them.

Sally poured out tea in saucerless cups on a cleared space on the rug-chest. 'I've brought cups for you and Robin, Mandy. And a slice of cake each. And I didn't forget that you prefer biscuits, Tom. Sugar for you, Robin? No? Then it's only Miss B that takes it.'

'What d'you think of Mermaid?' Rennie asked as soon as Miss Brandon came in, because she had heard the footsteps going up to the end of the passage and back.

'I don't really know what to make of her – oh, thank you, Sally; have you sugared it? – I think the bump looks rather bigger, and she seems a bit touchy about it, now. Not that I expect it's anything serious, but all the same, I think I'll have the vet look at her tomorrow, just to be on the safe side.' Miss Brandon stirred her tea thoughtfully and the steam misted up over her glasses. 'I've brought the bran,' she went on. 'Amelia didn't turn a hair. She came all the way up from Charterhill in top, without blowing at all: I really almost had to hold her back.'

At this point there was a sudden diversion because Miss

Brandon discovered that her tea tasted terribly of paraffin, though no-one else's did. Rennie raced up the wooden stairs to fetch her a clean cup, and Sally poured out more tea. The work began again with the muddy tack, and Rennie and Tom talked about the Colonel's colt, Templar, and Robin and Mandy began to argue about the best breed of dog. And then Miss Brandon announced in a doomed sort of voice that her second cup tasted of paraffin, and it was passed round like an exhibit at a lecture for everyone to smell and remark about.

'That smells more like metal-polish to me,' said Tom, with a connoisseur's sniff.

'But not in *two* cups,' said Miss Brandon disbelievingly. 'And I was so looking forward to my tea.'

Rennie tore up to the house again, carrying out a detailed private investigation which presently brought to light the sugar-packet and the metal-polish cosily pushed together on the same shelf, with the polish tin toppled on its side.

'Mrs Waddy must have been mad,' Sally said when Rennie came back with yet another cup, sugar from a new packet, and the explanation of the mystery. But Miss Brandon only wiped her glasses and said tolerantly that Mrs Waddy had been very absent-minded since she started doing football pools, because she was always so preoccupied in thinking what she would do with a fortune when she won one. 'But it's rather a shame about all that sugar,' she added wistfully. 'I don't suppose even Hall would look at it.'

'Hallmark's had a good-night sugar-lump every night for the last seventeen years,' Sally told Robin.

'He had a cup of tea and a meat-pie yesterday,' said Mandy. 'Really he did. I didn't want mine, and he asked for it, and so I gave it to him.'

'I haven't drunk mine!' said Robin, suddenly full of the idea; and somehow everybody was making for Hallmark's box and Mandy was urging Robin not to spill any tea, and Tom was telling them all about a flea-bitten grey he used to look after that had a pint of beer every Friday, and Miss Brandon was saying that it would come expensive if Hall was going to want a bedtime drink as well as his sugar-lump.

Hallmark drank the tea by scooping his tongue into the cup, cat-like, looking dreamy as he did so; and then he licked his lips in a slightly self-conscious manner when everyone said what a clever horse he was. Robin discovered Snowy curled down in a deep, small hole in Hallmark's straw, and was enchanted enough to remain behind wiggling straws over the brim while Tom went back to finish the last of the tack-cleaning and the others began feeding and watering and settling the horses for the night.

Miss Brandon always measured out the feeds, surrounding herself with as many buckets as there were horses and ponies in stables, and putting into each the special ingredients for different horses: a few sliced carrots on the top of the feed for Hallmark and Barbemusche and Mermaid, sugar-beet pulp for all except Jester – 'He doesn't like anything unusual' – cattle-nuts for a few that liked them and condition powders for Barbemusche – 'He never looks really well, that horse. I think it must be his nerves.'

Rennie sent Robin off home so that he would get back well before dark, sending with him loving messages to her father and Aunt Lucy, then she finished the haying and watering with Sally, trying not to think too much about Mermaid; but Miss Brandon went back to the tack-room to discuss the matter of Sir Richard with Tom Pigram, and finally decided to have the cob sent out on trial. 'He's docked but not hogged,' she was saying, 'and stands about sixteen-three.'

'Big, fer a cob,' said Tom, who was polishing stirrup-irons. 'That'll want some feeding.'

'I know. But if anything happens to Brown Jane we'll be properly up the gum-tree as far as the Major is concerned. And he's too good a client to lose.'

After supper she suddenly thought that if she telephoned to

arrange for Sir Richard's early departure the next morning, she could save a considerable sum by having the vet look over him when he came to see Mermaid. 'And I'll get him to look at Snowy too, just in case we were wrong when we decided he was a she. Because, if she is a he, after all, he will have to be Altered, and he's just about the age.'

The next morning was very full for Sally and Rennie, because Miss Brandon had the Three Graces, and Ann had their youngest client of all, a supremely confident three-year-old called Jane; so that there were only Sally and Rennie to greet the new cob when he arrived in a hired horse-box, and to establish him in the empty box next to Mermaid's, as well as to catch up ponies ready for the Lister children in the afternoon, and take three horses to the forge.

'And it looks as if Sir Richard will have to be shod, too, before he can do much work,' Sally said, looking at him critically through his open doorway. 'Doesn't he look funny with a mane and no tail.'

'He's awfully big,' said Rennie, 'but he has a nice head.'

'Farmer's perfect cob; pull the dung cart, plough and trap, and carry the farmer to hounds two days a week,' said Sally. 'Come on, we'll be late at the forge.'

They took the Stranger, Jester, Hallmark, and Spindle, with Sally riding Hallmark and leading the other three. Rennie drove Shamus in the trap behind them, so that she and Sally could get to the stables, leaving the horses with the blacksmith until they were ready to be fetched home.

'Hall's the best we've got, to lead from,' Sally said, mounting in the yard. 'He takes a kindly interest in all the other horses. Did you notice how he whickered a greeting to Sir Richard when we led him in? He always welcomes all the new ones. Now, give me Spindle's and Jester's reins ... thanks. All you have to do is to follow behind us, and keep a good horse's length between.'

It was a great thrill for Rennie to be driving Shamus entirely by herself, even at a gentle walk along Hampshire lanes and behind other horses. But Sally drove on the way home, keeping Shamus up to his best harness trot, with everything jingling and creaking and whirring in a most exhilarating manner.

'Your month's trial will soon be up,' she remarked, keeping her eyes on Shamus and the road. 'Are you going to stay on, d'you suppose?'

Rennie said doubtfully, 'I'd like to; but I don't know if I'll be asked.'

'Oh, you'll be asked all right. Miss B likes you. And you're getting pretty useful.' After a minute she added, 'You're not thinking of making a career of it, are you?'

'I don't know. I haven't thought that far. But I think it's the only thing I really want to do.'

'Well, I shouldn't, if I were you,' said Sally bluntly.

'But why not? You have. And so have Ann and Miss Brandon.'

'Oh, well, Ann and Miss B just can't keep away from horses; that's the way they both are. But I wouldn't like to think that I'd still be at it in another five years' time. The riding part is good fun, of course, but it simply doesn't pay. And think of the hours. No trade unions for riding-school people. I don't think *any*one – unless it's farmers – works the hours we do, or has less time off. Well, I ask you; one half-day a week and a whole day every other week.'

'But we do get lots of odd times off, when business is slack,' Rennie pointed out, watching Shamus's round back bobbing in the shafts.

'You can't plan anything, with odd times off.... And what future is there in it? Six pounds a week, all found, is about the most you can ever earn, for the rest of your life; or start a place of your own and have all the work and worry and financial crisis that go with it. Honestly, Rennie,' she added in a hushed voice that was almost lost under the clatter of Shamus's hoofs. 'I remember once, after a month's hard frost when all hunting and riding was cancelled, and Miss B told me that she had lost more than a hundred and fifty pounds.'

Rennie looked grave. A hundred and fifty pounds seemed such a colossal sum, and she was moved with compassion for Miss Brandon, for whom she had developed a great admiration. But she said, 'Six pounds a week, all found, doesn't seem very bad to me. And I don't expect either Ann or Miss B would want any other life, or why do they stick at this one?'

'Oh, it's all right if you're married to horses, I suppose,' said Sally airily, swinging Shamus past an approaching car.

'And you?' said Rennie; 'what are you going to do, then?'

'Me? Oh, I hope I'll be married, too, but not to horses!' said Sally. And then presently she added, as if one thing had led naturally to the other, 'Do you suppose – I wonder if Maurice's forgetting about horses has made him different in any other way? In his character, I mean.'

'I don't know,' said Rennie. 'I haven't thought about it very much.'

'Well, I'm glad to hear it,' said Sally, in the hard voice she had used before in talking about Maurice. 'But judging by the way he looks at you, I should think the reverse can't be true. We were once nearly engaged, you know,' she added in a distant sort of voice. 'Before the accident.'

'I know. I'm so sorry.' Rennie hardly knew what to say.

'I almost believe you,' said Sally. 'You're such a kid – but a nice one. All the same, I wish you weren't at Kingwood Stables,' she added honestly, and turned Shamus into his own stable-yard, where Ann had just arrived with the small three-year-old on Cobweb. While they were unharnessing Shamus and putting the trap away, Rennie could hear Ann absorbed in the teaching that she loved.

'Hold on to the saddle-tree – remember which the tree is, Jane? That's right! Now, swing your right leg over the cantle and slither to the ground. As easy as that! What do you do now? Not just drop your reins and walk away.... That's the idea; give Cobweb a pat and say thank you, and then lead him to his stable – and mind he doesn't tread on your heels!'

The Three Graces came in shortly afterwards with Miss Brandon on Barbemusche, and they all went straight to the spare loose-box to look at the new horse and comment on him.

'Oh, but Jean, he's such a *big* horse!'

'I can't see him in a side-saddle, Amy dear, can you?'

'Oh, Jean! do look at his funny little tail!'

'I expect he'll look better when he's clipped out,' said Miss Brandon, and gave him a lump of sugar from the pocket which always bulged with them. 'I hear that he has very good manners, and that's worth a great deal.'

The vet came during the afternoon when Rennie and Sally were out with Maurice and the Lister children. It was one of those days when Ann's 'mornings' had turned into afternoons as well, because one of the ponies had been getting very difficult and 'nappy', and she decided that it must have some schooling. 'The trouble is, there simply isn't time,' she said cheerfully, dashing out to the Park field with a halter. And so it was that Ann was still at Kingwood at tea-time and reported the vet's findings to the returning riders in her usual forthright manner, instead of Miss Brandon telling about it with her particular tact and serenity.

'I say, poor old Mermaid! She's got poll evil. Usually they die of it, of course, but Mr Simpson says he's going to have a go at operating. Sir Richard's sound except for a spavin – an old one; it won't affect him much, but he may wear his shoes hard at front. And Snowy's a tom, after all, and he's been de-tommed.'

Rennie felt as if someone had hit her across the face. No amount of reasoning with herself could remove the feeling that in some way she was responsible for Mermaid's state, and she led Dark Stranger, whom she had been riding, back to his box without a word. Her hand was shaking on his reins, and the Stranger, a sensitive animal, began at once to react with nervousness himself. He jumped at the sight of a perfectly ordinary stable barrow and broom in the passage, and made a great to-do about passing the new horse's box, with snortings and rollings of his eyes. Rennie, in her turn, began to dither more noticeably, and by the time she had got Stranger into his box they were both strung up to danger-point. Disliking her unsteady hand fumbling at his bridle, the black horse decided that he couldn't bear the tension any longer and suddenly snapped at her. Rennie wasn't hurt, but the shock on top of the shock about Mermaid was too much, and she swung sharply away from him; but somehow her hand was caught under one rein and gave Dark Stranger a mighty jerk in his mouth. The horse opened his eyes very wide, laid his ears back flat along his head, and snorted. And then he suddenly grasped the back of Rennie's jersey in his teeth and flung her violently out of his box.

When Ann and Miss Brandon got to the end of the passage they found Rennie huddled limply on the ground and the Stranger shivering in a cold sweat by the open door of his box.

# 10 | For the Life Itself

'I HAVEN'T f-fainted,' said Rennie apologetically, 'but I c-can't get up.'

Miss Brandon gently sat her up on the stone floor while Ann shut the Stranger's door; and then Sally and Maurice were there and the two young Listers.

'We'd better carry her upstairs, I think,' said Miss Brandon. 'Ann, you and Maurice are the strongest . . . and Sally, will you dash up and get the kettle on? Some strong tea will help, I daresay . . . John and Janet, would you like to carry on down here, filling up water-buckets? That really would be a help.'

'I'm so s-sorry,' said Rennie weakly, looking at her hands, which were so useless, and a wave of bleak despair came slowly over her.

'Well, stop being sorry then!' said Ann with sympathetic briskness as she took hold of Rennie's legs. 'Really, it's we that are sorry for you. Ready, Maurice? Up she rises, then!'

'Whatever could have come over old Stranger?' Miss Brandon said in a puzzled voice, following them down the passage and under Hallmark's querying muzzle.

When they got Rennie safely into her bedroom and Maurice had been firmly sent back to help the children in the stables, Ann and Miss Brandon carefully undressed their patient. They found a raw red place across her shoulder-blades and the marks of Stranger's teeth. Miss Brandon washed and dressed the wound with her usual quiet efficiency, and helped Rennie to drink some of Sally's tea before she telephoned Rennie's own doctor, who said that he would look in after tea.

Meanwhile, Rennie slowly came back to life again, lying alone in her room while the others were rushing through the last of the stable jobs without her. She flexed her fingers, staring at them thoughtfully, and moved her feet under the blankets. She was all right, then. The weakness had passed. Really, there was no need to go on lying there, she thought, when other people were doing her work....

Pushing back the bedclothes, Rennie put out her feet and stood up; but only for a second. In no more time than that, she was huddled on the floor again and quite unable to rise by her own effort. She was still there, wrapped round in a blanket that she had pulled from the bed, when Sally and Miss Brandon came up again an hour or so later for their own tea; and she only said, 'Yes, I know,' in a sad, small voice when they told her how rash she had been. And then she added bleakly, 'Is Mermaid really very ill? Does Mr Simpson think she has a good chance?'

'A sporting chance, I suppose,' said Miss Brandon. 'He's a very good vet.' Then she suddenly turned and looked at Rennie again thoughtfully. 'What did Ann say to you, when you were leading Stranger in?'

Rennie had physical weaknesses that most other people didn't have, but she had more perception than most people, too, almost as if it had been given to her in compensation. She only replied, 'That Mr Simpson was going to operate,' but the words 'they usually die of it, of course' were standing inside her mind.

'Well—' Sally began, as if to add to this, but something in Rennie's face stopped her. Not that it would have mattered, she supposed, since everyone can't be expected to have skill and tact with nervous cases; but all the same...

Rennie's doctor found no physical injury except the wound in the back, but he was not encouraging about the set-back in her nervous illness.

'At least a week in bed; probably more,' he said. 'And it must be complete rest, preferably not within earshot of other people's busy-ness. It would be better, really, if she went home.'

Rennie's look of absolute hopelessness at this touched Miss Brandon's generous nature. 'She could stay here, very gladly, if she liked. The only thing is that I'm afraid there would never be time to nurse her properly. She'd be left on her own almost all of the time, except at meals.'

'And there'd be terrible sounds of busy-ness,' Sally pointed out, secretly hoping that Rennie would, in fact, soon be out of her – and Maurice's – way.

Miss Brandon was not herself ill-equipped in matters of perception, and she had a fair idea of what was gnawing in Rennie's mind. 'Of course, you'll soon be back again,' she said, 'if you do go home for a while. We can't let you stay away for long, you know! In fact, I was going to offer you a proper job, when your month's trial was up.'

'Really, she will be able to work again much sooner,' said the doctor, 'if she does have a week or so at home.'

Rennie nodded, content now to agree to go anywhere, even back to hospital, if it would get her well any sooner.

'I'll call in and explain everything to your family, on my way home,' the doctor said. 'Shall I tell them to expect you to-morrow?'

Rennie nodded again. 'Thank you.'

'And tell Robin, will you,' said Miss Brandon, 'that he needn't feel he's got to stay away till Rennie's better. Even a week's a long time, when you're only ten.'

For ten days Rennie lay in bed at home, not even allowed to write a letter: but she received several from Kingwood Riding School, even including a sympathetic note from Mrs Waddy; and until Robin went back to school she had regular news from him. The most important news of all to Rennie was the news of Mermaid's operation for poll evil.

'Mr Simpson was really wonderful, considering the difficulties here,' Miss Brandon wrote. 'The chloroform was administered in a nose-bag, out in the lower paddock, and Sally and I were surgeon's assistants. Mermaid came through it very well, but we aren't sure yet whether the operation has been successful or not. Mandy sends her love, and so do Finner and Fatter and Jane and the Three Graces. We all miss you very much, so hurry up and get well soon.'

Miss Brandon followed up her letter by coming to tea in the second week, as soon as Rennie was allowed to get up for it. She drove herself over in Amelia, looking quite like another younger, gayer person in a soft brown skirt and yellow jersey, and she got on so well with Aunt Lucy and Rennie's father – widely different though they were – that Rennie almost began to feel as if she were one of the family. While Aunt Lucy made the tea, they discussed Rennie's future together, and Miss Brandon said much the same sort of things that Sally had said to Rennie, driving home from the forge.

'There isn't really much money in riding; except perhaps in schooling, and in a few very big, specialized stables, and in dealing, of course. I could have made money in dealing, myself, but I don't like to touch it. The dealing that really pays isn't usually honest dealing.'

'I suppose money is only a symbol for most people's ideas of happiness,' Mr Jordan said thoughtfully. 'What about riding, then, from the point of view of the life itself?'

'Oh, well,' Miss Brandon said, smiling, 'for people who love horses, it's almost the only life! Of course, the work is really hard, and the hours are long; but nobody minds working long hours at the thing they like doing best.'

Rennie's father looked at his daughter quizzically. 'And do you like doing it as much as that?'

Rennie smiled too, at both of them. 'After all that's happened,' she said, 'I think I must really know my own mind when I say yes!'

After another week of convalescence, which included a visit with Robin and her father to the stables, Rennie returned to Kingwood; but this time as a girl-groom, receiving one pound a week and her keep. 'And at the end of the winter,' Miss Brandon said, 'if all goes well, I'll double it; and treble it by next autumn. You might work up to six pounds or so, eventually, if you get really good, but that would be about the top limit here. You might earn much more, perhaps, if you got into a good showing or breeding establishment, or with a racing stables, say, or schooling young horses – a most satisfying job, that, I think. But you would have to be quite top class for work like that. Some dealers, too, pay enormous money compared with ours. But I think it's mostly based on other people's disappointments.'

It was mid-October, and Rennie came back to a busy stables on the brink of another hunting season. Sir Richard was still there, having tempted Miss Brandon to buy him for the sake of Major Cornelius; Barbemusche was still laying his ears back sourly in the stable, in his usual embittered manner, and having condition powders and tit-bits on his feed; and Hallmark was still enjoying his good-night sugar-lumps, as well as an occasional cup of warm, sweet tea and somebody's sandwich. Rennie looked at them all with joyful delight in reunion, even including a visit to the sinister Dark Stranger, who now flapped his lower lip in a dreamy manner as if nothing would induce him to make unkind advances at anyone. She exclaimed about the enormous size of Puffin's puppies, and the way Snowy had grown, and then finally she went to see Mermaid. She had left this to the last, with a kind of reluctant disbelief in the latest news – that Mermaid had not responded to the operation as well as had been hoped, and was to undergo a second one very shortly.

She looked much the same to Rennie, except that she was

thinner, and she whickered a friendly greeting that twisted Rennie's heart, considering the cause of her dire illness.

'Mr Simpson says that she was so courageous,' Sally told her in the loose-box, stroking Mermaid, 'that he simply had to pull her through, if it could possibly be done. He opened up one side of her head – the side away from you – and next week he will open the other. He says we must all go on fighting for her, so long as there is anything we can do.'

Life and work at the stables went on exactly the same as usual after Rennie's return, but under it all, like a current running under a tide, was the general anxiety and preoccupation about Mermaid.

When the day and the hour arrived for her second ordeal, she was as quiet and sensible as if she had no knowledge at all of what the vet and his strange-smelling bag must mean to her. 'But she knows, of course,' said Miss Brandon, leading her out from the covered yard. 'Horses are very slow to learn, compared with humans, but, unlike humans, they never forget anything they once knew.'

Rennie had wanted to help at the operation, because, though she shrank from the very idea of it, she felt that it was one small thing she could do to help make up for being the cause of Mermaid's plight. But Miss Brandon wisely refused, saying that it would be easier for Mr Simpson to have the same assistants as before, and so it would be better for Mermaid, too. Instead, she sent Rennie out on Spindle with Maurice Lowe, who was no longer accompanied by John and Janet now that the Michaelmas term had started. The sight of them riding away together, on the top of the anxiety about Mermaid, plunged Sally into a state of gloom that lasted until the end of that day. It was the first time that Rennie had ridden with Maurice alone, and the worry of it affected Sally's efficiency as a 'theatre nurse' enough for Mr Simpson to tell her sharply to 'wake up'.

Sally was not an unduly imaginative person: her fears about Maurice were based on sound observation and a long acquaintance with Maurice himself. She knew that he was fascinated by Rennie and her determination to regain her health in the one way she believed possible.

Rennie herself half guessed at the way things were, but she generally tried not to think about it; partly because she faithfully looked on Maurice as Sally's property, and partly because she wanted neither Maurice nor anyone else to complicate still further her already complicated life. She was very young, and in many ways she was younger than her years. But, above all, she wanted to straighten out the present problems of her life before she added any further ones. She knew Maurice fairly well by now, from frequent rides in his company, and enjoyed his amusing conversation and mature but youthful outlook. Neither of them ever spoke about the particular maladjustments that had set them both riding, until Maurice suddenly said on this late October afternoon: 'We're pretty much the same, aren't we, you and I? A couple of crocks on life's scrap-heap.'

Rennie had been tightening Spindle's girth – he was still out at grass and shrank unbelievably when on a ride. 'Oh, I don't know,' she said in a preoccupied way. 'I may be a crock, but I don't think I'm on a scrap-heap, yet. Shall we turn down through the woods, or go over the common?'

As she spoke, looking down through the quiet beauty of the woodland ride all hung with gold and flame, Rennie felt a catch in her throat. The contrast between the woodland's lovely serenity and her own aching disquiet was too great.

Distantly, she heard Maurice say: 'You sound as if you haven't got your mind on the matter, so it may as well be the woods.'

'I haven't,' Rennie said, 'it's on Mermaid. The more I try to stop thinking about her, the more I keep wondering what's happening to her, now.'

Maurice opened the gate into the woods, leaning down from Julia's saddle. 'And to think I half hoped that it might have been on me!' he said lightly, watching her ride through. Rennie blushed, and hated herself for doing so. She wanted to make some clever, crushing, and wise remark, but couldn't think of anything to say at all. Maurice had shut the gate and was riding beside her again. He said, a little wickedly because he knew she was ruffled, 'I wish I could think of things to say that would keep you blushing all the time. I can't tell you how it suits you!'

Rennie made Spindle walk faster, and looked fixedly at his pointed ears. She said in a low voice, 'You're not being fair to Sally.'

Maurice didn't answer for a moment, and then he said quite seriously. 'I know I'm not. But, Rennie, I can't think about Sally when you're here. We're – we're so much *alike,* you and I. You must have realized it, yourself.'

'I haven't,' said Rennie wretchedly. 'Can't you see that I've got enough difficulties to deal with, without wanting to stir up any more?'

Maurice said humbly, 'I'm sorry, Rennie! But ... don't you think that someone else – like me, perhaps – who knows a bit about those difficulties of yours because of having had them himself, might be able to help you deal with them? I hate to think of you, battling on alone. Truly, Rennie, I'm very serious.'

Rennie went on looking straight ahead, sitting very erect in her saddle. 'No, Maurice, I don't think so. I don't think that anyone can help me, now, except myself. And I think that two nervous people together would make each other worse than they were before. And I'm too young. And there is Sally. And all I can think of at the moment is Mermaid.... I'm sorry if that sounds silly to you, but it was all sort of my fault, and – do you mind if we canter here? I want to get back and see how she is.'

# 11 'Wanted, Good Girl with Horses'

Through the next week Rennie was anxious and preoccupied, both about Mermaid and about her own effect on Sally's friendship with Maurice. The riding-school was very busy, which was a good thing in the circumstances. Most of the horses were being clipped out ready for hunting, and Rennie learned to use the electric clippers on easy horses like Flossie and Brown Jane, while Ann dealt in her efficient way with the really bad ones like Jester and Barbemusche.

'I hate putting a twitch on him,' Ann said, twisting the narrow rope round Jester's muzzle, 'but it really is his own fault. He just won't stand still without it. He's a funny horse; funny to look at, with that spotted coat, and in his character, too. He's scared of his own skin, almost. The moment you want to do anything for him he panics.'

Rennie had the job of holding the twitch while Ann drove the whirring clippers through Jester's circus-coloured coat. Horse-hair floated about the covered yard on the breeze from the open double-doors and made Rennie's nose tickle. She said: 'I'm glad I'm doing Brown Jane next, and not this one. She's rather nice.'

'She used not to be. She was a complaining sort of horse when we first had her. She moped all the time. But she's much better now. Talking of moping,' Ann suddenly added, running the clippers down Jester's lowered neck, 'what's the matter with Sally these days? It's as much as one dare do to say anything to her.'

Rennie was just going to say, 'I don't know'; but of course she did know, and she hesitated long enough for Ann to glance at her suspiciously.

'It's you and Maurice.'

'Maurice, perhaps,' said Rennie, 'but not me. I mean, I haven't done anything at all, except just be here.'

'I saw it coming, weeks ago,' said Ann. 'From the time you arrived, in fact.'

Rennie suddenly felt extremely sorry for herself, in a way she rarely did. 'I don't know why,' she said tragically, 'but everything dreadful has to happen to me. Right from the time I was small, until now. It makes you understand the way people used to believe in malevolent gods. Even here, where I really was happy and getting so much better and everything, it's all been spoiled, and I know I shall have to try to find somewhere else.'

Ann pushed the clippers into the stubs of Jester's hogged mane. 'Don't be silly,' she said. 'Love isn't all that much important. I've been in and out of it three times myself, and every time I thought I was going to die of heart-break. But now I'm twenty-eight I know how tough the human heart is.'

Rennie said, 'But Sally's only eighteen, and hers isn't tough.'

As the days passed into November, Miss Brandon began to be optimistic about Mermaid's recovery. On fine days Rennie would lead the mare for exercise, rugged up but with the operation scar hideously open to the sun and air, the soft hair clipped away all round it so that it could be kept clean by daily antiseptic swabbings. Rennie particularly enjoyed these walks with Mermaid, because there seemed to be a kind of affinity with a led horse that was not the same when one was riding. And sometimes Puffin would come with them, too; a thing she never did with ridden horses. Leading Mermaid, Rennie could dawdle along and absorb the glorious abandon of November leaf-colour, the leaves hanging golden above and falling golden through the air, to lie in a shining, rustling carpet under her and Mermaid's leisurely feet.

On three mornings a week, now, horses from the stables went out hunting. This meant very early rising, and hard work trimming tails and plaiting manes beforehand, and harder work cleaning muddy horses and mountains of mud-plastered tack afterwards. Rennie was far too much of a novice to go hunting herself in her first winter, but once or twice she rode and led horses some miles to a meet for clients who were arriving there by car. It was very exciting; the arrival of the van-load of hounds, all with their muzzles pressed to the slatted sides; the pink-coated huntsmen on magnificent hunt horses; the children on trace-clipped ponies watched by anxious parents or friends on bigger horses; and the crowd of lookers-on with prams and bicycles and cars.

Rennie would usually be on Shamus, with whom she had learned to lead horses while mounted; and when she and Ann or Sally had handed over their charges they would ride back down the quiet lanes to the stables and carry on the work where they had left it. Now and again, when Mrs Waddy was not too pressed indoors, she would toil wheezily down the wooden steps at eleven o'clock with a tray of tea for anyone who was not out riding; and with the tea she would dispense a news commentary on grandchildren, football pools, and Miss Brandon's health – a thing that always worried her because 'there's no one else, well is there, to worry for her? And she never thinks about herself, and that's a fact. I wish she had a nice sensible partner, now, what'd take a bit of the burden from her.'

'Poor Miss B!' said Ann when they were saddling up ponies for the boys from Kingwood School. 'I don't suppose she would think of affording a partner. Do you know, she's only charging sixpence an hour more than the average charges ten years ago?

And all her expenses must be up about three times as much. It's a skilled business, making a riding-school pay in these days. . . . Heavens! Is that the boys arriving already? Throw me that bridle over, Rennie, quick, and you can take Cobweb and Jenny Wren and Shamus.'

It was fun going out on Spindle with Ann and the boys from Kingwood School. This particular class was of boys about ten years old, and Ann was at her best teaching them. They had all the cowboy stuff of swinging lariats and turning in the saddle, done at the walk and trot; and there was an exhilarating company canter down a grassy ride between high, golden hedges, with Ann in front and Rennie in the rear of the class. One boy, a dark, Italian-looking youngster with a very swashbuckling manner, came tumbling off Snowcloud's back and over his shoulder as they pulled up near the end of the track. Ann was out of the Stranger's saddle in a second and making sure that he was all right; and, having assured herself that he was, encouraging him to get up by himself and catch Snowcloud and remount.

'You know why you fell, don't you?' she said to him. 'It was because your hands were too high. You held them up here, and then you followed them. You'll always follow your hands, you'll find. Keep them down here, close to the saddle, and you'll stay there with them.' Afterwards she said to Rennie, 'It's a funny thing, but people like that, who have a bold manner, are always much more upset by a fall than the quieter ones are.'

Coming to a clearing at the side of the track, Rennie saw a cleared circle in the copse, like a little circus ring, and there was a very low jump of brushwood to one side of it.

'This is where they have their very first jumping lessons,' Ann told her. 'It's only about nine inches high, and they hardly notice it.'

She marshalled the ponies in a long line and sent them off one by one round the ring and over the jump, except for two who had said they would rather not start jumping till next term. Ann stood in the middle of the circle like a ring-master, and praised, encouraged, instructed, or helped as need required, while Rennie held Dark Stranger's reins. The boys were all enjoying themselves enormously, because jumping was jumping, even if it was only on a very small scale; and presently the first of the two non-jumpers had joined the line and taken the brushwood very neatly.

'Good fellow, John!' Ann called out. 'I thought you weren't going to try until next term. My word, the term's gone fast!'

And then the second boy was jumping too, and no one wanted to stop when Ann said that the ponies had had enough.

Rennie enjoyed this class more than the classes of older boys, who were more staid and polite but less full of excitement and zest. There were fewer older boys riding, too, and some of them seemed to be doing it more as a matter of form than for pure pleasure or a love of horses. But one boy, Morgan Davy, was different because he had an absolute passion for horses; and because of his great interest he had learned to ride really well. He was a Welsh boy, about Rennie's own age, and planning to be a farmer when he grew up, and to keep horses for work and pleasure on the farm. He and Rennie talked endlessly about the future farm on these school rides: where it would be, how big, and of what type; whether to go in for sheep on the hills, or arable on the rich lowlands, or beef or dairy cattle on good grassland; or whether, perhaps, to emigrate after all, and farm in New Zealand or Australia?

Rennie began to be almost as much absorbed in Morgan's farm as he was himself, and she knew that when she left Kingwood these cloud-castle conversations would be one of the things that she would lose with regret. And she knew, now, that when opportunity presented itself she would – she must – leave Kingwood. Sally was hardly on speaking terms with her any more, and this was not really to be wondered at, considering how Maurice sought her out whenever he came riding, having nothing for Sally now except a casual friendly greeting.

At least, there was the relief and joy of knowing that Mermaid really was getting better, and would not die of poll evil, as so many good horses had done. Rennie was glad to think that she wouldn't have to leave Kingwood without knowing what the little skewbald's fate was going to be.

November had given place to December, with long days of work and anxiety, of fun and delight – rides with Robin and Mandy, and Finner and Fatter, with the three elderly ladies and the schoolboys, and with new clients who had seen Miss Brandon's cinema-screen advertisement – before Rennie made herself face the fact that opportunity was not going to present itself, and that she must find it for herself. A little sadly, she began to study the Situations Vacant column in Miss Brandon's *Horse and Hound*, and it was there that she found Mr Joe Gallon.

'Wanted, good girl with horses', his advertisement read; 'need not have much experience, but willing to learn. Excellent wages and prospects for right girl. Apply Joe Gallon, Silver Horseshoe Stables, Bentley, Nr. Leicester.'

This was the only advertisement that did not specify skill and experience, and it was the only one that seemed to have both good wages and prospects to offer.

Rennie applied, being perfectly honest and straightforward about her illness, but saying how much better she had been in recent weeks. And, the following day being a day off, she went home by the country bus and explained everything to her father and Aunt Lucy.

Aunt Lucy was, not unnaturally, against any idea of change at all. 'Considering all that Miss Brandon has done for you and how well you've got on with her. I don't know how you can consider it, Rennie. After all, as you aren't encouraging this Maurice person, I don't see what Sally can object to in your just being there.'

Rennie sighed a little. 'But it's my just being there that she does object to.' It was very difficult trying to explain things like this to the middle-aged.

But Rennie's father had an objection from quite an unexpected viewpoint. He had, he told her, applied for a vacant position on the staff of Kingwood School, and he was now almost sure of getting it. 'It's a better job than my present one, and more interesting, too. But the thing that particularly attracted me about it was its nearness to the riding-school. I haven't told Robin yet, of course, but he will be delighted, now he's so often at the stables; and I had thought how nice it was going to be, having you so near us again. I even thought of doing a bit of riding, myself, now and again . . . it doesn't do to get into a rut.'

'Oh, Dad! I am so sorry!' Rennie said. 'It would have been such fun. Will you be living at the school, do you think?'

'There's a pleasant little cottage in the grounds that goes with the job. I think it used to be a staff cottage in the days of the Great House. No more long bicycle rides twice a day!' He, too, sighed a little, staring into the smouldering fire. 'If you must leave Kingwood, Rennie, why go so far away? Couldn't you try for a job at one of the other local stables?'

'Oh, Dad – you know it wouldn't be any use. After all, I'd be at Kingwood with you quite a lot, and then Maurice has a car. Besides, somehow, I sort of feel I want to see if I can be quite independent, now. And I do terribly want to be able to meet *all* my own expenses, and have a bit left to send home, too – to make up for all I've been costing you. And this job looks like being a fairly well-paid one.'

'You can forget all about sending money home,' said Mr Jordan, definitely. 'If you ever do such a thing, my lass, I shall just bank it for you.' Looking at her in a wistful way that snatched at her heart, he added, 'I wish it wasn't working out like this.'

Rennie was torn. Even Aunt Lucy seemed sorry that she might be going.

'Perhaps, when Sally's got over it, I may come back to Kingwood one day. But I must go away, now. Oh dear, I am so sorry!'

# 12 | Plain Psychology

Replying to Rennie's detailed letter, Joe Gallon sent her a terse but business-like note describing his Silver Horseshoe Stables as a 'high-class dealing establishment, just outside the town', and offering her the job at a starting wage of four pounds a week, all found, 'and I can double it any day, if you turn out to be as good as I think you will'. His wife, he said, was willing to accommodate Rennie in the farmhouse.

Mr Jordan was insistent on an interview, and went up with Rennie himself to see Mr Gallon and his stables. The place itself was really a small grazing farm, now turned over almost entirely to horses and ponies. The fields and buildings seemed full of them – all kinds and sizes and conditions. The stone house seemed clean enough, though not very homelike, and it was littered with dogs and cats and puppies lying in heaps around the hearth. Mrs Gallon made them a pot of tea, and bustled about in a chronically anxious manner that Mr Jordan feared would not do Rennie much good; but Joe himself was a big, red, blustering man, who radiated energy and drive.

'I started here as a dairy farmer, you know,' he told Mr Jordan expansively, 'but I soon found out where the money was. All the cows I got here now will likely be sold within the month, same as the dogs and horses. Mind you, you got to know the ropes to make a go of dealing – same as with any business. You got to know where to lay your hands on things cheap, and where to get rid of 'em dear. I got into this just after the War, and now I reckon I know as much about it as anyone in the country.'

Rennie, it seemed, would have no stable work at all to do, being only required to exercise the horses and ponies, to do some trimming and clipping and to attend sales with Mr Gallon. But especially she was wanted to show off animals to potential customers. 'Nothing influences a customer more than seeing a really nice young lady showing off a horse's points and paces. Gives 'em confidence, you know, as nothing else will. Same when you can advertise, "Ridden by a lady". Ar, you learn a lot about human nature in my job, I can tell you, Mr Jordan, sir. All the same, we got a lot of good regular customers as come again and again, and you can't say more for a business than that, now can you?'

Mr Jordan decided that though he did not want Rennie to go to the Silver Horseshoe Stables, he could not think of any very adequate reason why. In the train on the way home they talked it over.

'I don't know what it is about him, quite, Rennie. Perhaps it's just that he doesn't strike me as being very genuine. And I think you may find Mrs Gallon a bit wearing, too.'

Rennie frowned a little, thinking about it all, and wishing suddenly that she need never leave Kingwood. After a minute she said, 'I think, Dad, that if you don't definitely say I mustn't, I'll give it a trial. After all, I can try it for, say, a couple of months, and then see what I think of it. Anything can happen in a couple of months. Sally might even marry Maurice; you never know.'

Everyone except Sally, it seemed, was sorry to think of Rennie going. Miss Brandon was genuinely disappointed that Rennie felt she could not stay, but with her broad human understanding she had seen the way things were, and did not attempt to belittle the situation, as Ann had done. 'But if you're ever in need of a job again, Rennie,' she said, 'you know where we are. Just drop me a line.'

Ann was both impatient and sorry. 'You are a coot, really, Rennie! You'll never get as good a place as this, again. Unless you're thinking only of money, of course, and I'll admit that's suspiciously plentiful where you're going.'

Sally only said, 'Oh, well, think of us, toiling away with barrows and dung-forks, when you're elegantly showing off horses. Fancy! no stable work at all.'

Maurice seemed so badly shocked at the news that he hardly spoke to Rennie at all, after one impassioned plea to her to leave everything and marry him at once. 'There isn't anything else in the whole world that I want any more, except only just you.'

But the only thing that Rennie wanted in all the world was a kind of spiritual freedom in which to sort out her own life.

Morgan Davy had only said, 'Oh, well, I shall miss you. No one else has ever been so interested in my farm, and it was fun talking about it.' But people whom Rennie felt she hardly knew properly at all were touchingly sorry to say good-bye to her; even the terrifying Major Cornelius, whom she had only ever seen drive up in a tearing hurry on a hunting morning and pound away on Sir Richard to the meet. 'Sorry to lose you, my gel! Been nice seeing you around the place – nice – yes – oh, well —'

'You'll write and tell me about everyone and everything, won't you?' Rennie said to Miss Brandon. 'Where Puffin's puppies go, and any news from Tom about Templar, and if Mrs Waddy wins at football pools and especially how Mermaid is.'

Miss Brandon promised, and Rennie went to look round all the horses for the last time, with a clutching sense of sadness.

She arrived at Leicester station on a day of sudden frost in early January. Joe Gallon was on the platform and took her cases in a masterful manner, striding ahead of her to the barrier and talking all the time about her journey and the weather and the nice tea that Mrs Gallon had waiting for her. Outside the station he threw the luggage into the back of a very shiny and opulent estate car, and opened the door for Rennie with an exaggerated flourish.

'It pays to have a nice bus,' he said, getting in beside her. 'Does the business good, you know. And a business like mine can afford to carry it. Teach you to drive, too, shall I? Well you'll soon be eighteen; time you learned. Besides, it'd be darn useful to me if you could run about to the station and sales and that. I'll soon have you knowing a bit of good horseflesh when you see it – or how to make a bad bit look good, eh?' He suddenly laughed, clapping his hands down on the wheel.

Rennie found that she was not expected to say a great deal herself; only to listen to this big, gusty man talking. He could keep up a running flow of lively conversation through miles of driving or riding, she soon discovered, and though some of it was boring and distasteful, it was often amusing and very informative as well. He was such a big man that he seemed to overflow every place he was in. The large estate car seemed too small for him, and the spacious farmhouse appeared to shrink at his entry, and to shake and creak a little at his step. On horseback, Joe Gallon dwarfed even his heavyweight hunters – Sir Richard would have been quite eclipsed, Rennie thought with a homesick pang for Kingwood – and this was one reason why he was so pleased to have Rennie.

'Just what we need,' he said; 'a nice little lightweight that can ride the small ones. We'll have you hunting, too, before the season's out; oh, you needn't do any jumping and that. There's more ways of following hounds than one. But it does put up a horse's value when you can say "hunted by a lady" – stands to reason.'

Rennie loved dogs and cats, but she did find the numbers in the farmhouse rather overwhelming; and so did poor Mrs Gallon, judging by the martyred way in which she climbed around and over them, peering down in the winter darkness to see just where they all were. 'Oh, well, often a customer takes a fancy to one or another of them, when they come indoors to sign the cheque over a drink or two,' said Joe, and he would sit by the fire and stretch out his legs, resting his stockinged feet on any creatures that chanced to be handy.

Before breakfast the next morning he took Rennie round the stables and paddocks. All the old farm-buildings – even the pigsties and barn – had been adapted for accommodating something to sell, but mostly they were full of horses and ponies. Miss Brandon would have been horrified, Rennie thought, to see the tiny space allotted to each animal, and most of them tied by the head in the old-fashioned way.

'It's a bit cramped,' Joe admitted, 'but they aren't here for long, and we haven't any room for loose-boxes. Besides, with strings of strange horses coming in, it's as well to have them all properly secured.'

There were perhaps a couple of dozen animals in the buildings, not including a mixed herd of milking cows, some still with the market numbers pasted on their rumps. 'Gallon's the name for cattle in these parts,' Joe said proudly, 'and gallons are what they give the customer! One day you can work out a nice little slogan for me out of that, eh, Rennie? Now, in the paddocks we have the main part of our stock – horses and cattle.' He opened the yard gate for her and led her down a narrow lane to where gates led, at right and left, to wide, bare, wintry-looking paddocks on whose sparse grazing wisps of trampled hay blew in the wind. There were perhaps another forty or fifty animals in these fields; as rough a collection as Rennie had ever seen. They stood about in huddled groups under the hedges, out of the wind, and lifted their heads inquiringly when Rennie and Joe Gallon looked over the gates at them.

'They're rough as you like, now, of course,' said Joe, blowing on his fingers, 'but you'd be surprised what we can do with them inside of one short day. Say – someone rings up to ask have we got a nice lady's hunter, bay with black points, carry a side-saddle, ride or drive? I say sure we have, come along to-morrow! Now, you see that little mare over there, behind them two greys – the one with a small white saddle-mark? You say she looks rough enough now, I daresay? Just like any gippo's nag? Well, I tell you I could get her up to look like the Royal Mews by this time tomorrow! You'll see. There's some I keep in, ready for a quick sale like; but there's a lot more I keep up my sleeve, so to speak, and fetch up as required.'

The telephone rang several times during breakfast, which was a very well-cooked and ample one on proper farmhouse lines. Joe answered it himself the first time or two, noting down the customer's requirements and fixing appointments – he never seemed to mind in the least getting up in the middle of his meal – but presently he asked Rennie to answer any further calls for him.

'It makes a real impression on a client to hear a nice educated lady's voice at the other end,' he explained, helping himself to more bacon. 'Whatever they ask for, say you think we've got just the thing, and make notes of what they ask for in the book. Always try to fix an appointment if you can, but always for the next day, unless you know we've got the right one in the stables. We'll be trimming, this morning, so you'll soon get to know what we've got, where. Tell you what, though! Fast as you get to know 'em they'll be gone, God willing, and a new lot coming in!' He suddenly guffawed loudly, gesticulating cheerfully with his fork. 'We've got a sale on Wednesday, and another on Friday. You'll soon learn. And if you're a good girl, I'll raise your money. I can afford to. A good business can always carry good labour.'

He talked on, eating vastly all the while; and Rennie listened, and ate her own small breakfast between telephone conversations at the big leather-topped desk: 'Yes, this is the Silver Horseshoe Stables speaking. A child's first pony? Preferably grey, traffic proof, live out, easy to catch. . . .' She was writing it all down, her neat round hand looking very demure under Joe's big, sprawling one. 'I think we have just what you want. Would you like to come and see it tomorrow? Well, any time after nine, I think. Yes, that would do nicely....'

Then it was a couple of good Shorthorn down-calvers, and then a man who wanted a second-hand wagon, and finally a hack for a nervous lady. With each fresh inquiry Joe Gallon expanded a little more genially. Business did him more good than any tonic, and presently poor Mrs Gallon was clearing away the dishes and Joe was ushering Rennie out to the stables again.

The two men he employed for all the rougher work had finished the mucking-out and feeding and grooming, and were engaged on carting hay to the paddocks. Walking alertly down the lines of stabled animals with Rennie, Joe looked at them with a critical eye in relation to the day's visitors and inquiries.

'That black horse, there; he was out, as rough as the rest, this time yesterday. Gentleman coming to try him for jumping this morning. And that piebald pony, next but two; he was another. Covered in mud, they was, and hung with coats like door-mats.'

Rennie simply could not believe it. Both animals looked, now, like well-kept stabled favourites, with shiny, clipped coats, trimmed tails, and neatly plaited manes. They wore smart red-braided rugs, and their black-oiled hoofs were sunk in clean yellow straw.

'That kind of thing makes a real impression,' Joe Gallon said again. 'It's surprising what a lick of paint can do; but business is all plain psychology, really: you've got to understand the human mind. Now – today's inquiries: we can do the veg. cob and the lady's hack out of the stables, but we shall have to catch up the pony from the paddocks. You shall show off both the riding animals, Rennie; you're a nice light weight for that kind of job. Don't let yourself run to fat, now, whatever you do! I shall have to speak to Ethel about all that bacon – I lost my last two girls from running to fat. Near as big as me, they got, and that don't do at all in the horse business.' He reached for a couple of rope halters from a rack by the stable-door. 'Come along, now, and we'll weed out the two we want. And, God willing, there'll be at least another one wanted by lunch-time.'

# 13 | 'It Makes an Impression'

RENNIE was absorbed into the strange, swift world of horse-dealing from the dawn of her first day. Not that horses were the only stock-in-trade at the Silver Horseshoe Stables; Joe Gallon dealt in almost anything that could come in cheap and go out dear, as he had said. He had a shed full of second-hand saddlery, another full of all kinds of implements from a chaff-cutter to a tractor; he had stable-rugs and hen-coops, dogs and cows, three goats and a dozen fancy bantams; in fact, he could supply at once, or obtain quickly, almost anything a customer might ask for. He would sell the furniture out of his house, if anyone fancied it and the price was right; and he knew just where to lay his hands on suitable replacements.

At first, Rennie found the life exciting and full of fascination. She learned how to work very quickly and immaculately, and could soon turn out a smart-looking pony that had, only eight hours previously, been rough and muddy in the paddocks. Her riding improved enormously in the first week or two, with backing so many different kinds of horses and ponies, and she acquired a great confidence in handling them. She learned not to feel a pang of sorrow when a personal favourite was sold; and she learned, though with deep stabs of conscience, to say nothing about a horse's known faults and vices when a customer was at hand. This came particularly hard to Rennie when the buyer was young or in any way nervous, and she sometimes lapsed into a state of remorseful anxiety when she had had to assist in the sale of a totally unsuitable mount to such a person.

Joe Gallon had many tricks and dodges for 'improving' unlikely animals, both horses and cattle, but these he wisely kept secret from Rennie for as long as he could. He was a shrewd man, and fairly soon realized that she was not one who would wholly approve of some of his stratagems. Her shocked look when she came on him filing a horse's teeth one day was proof enough of that, even without his quite penetrating knowledge of humanity to help him. 'Oh, well, it just makes 'em look a bit younger, you know – only a year or so. Doesn't really make any difference, as you might say, but you got to appeal to the customer, haven't you? Like doing up the knitting wool in cellophane, and all that!'

One had to admit, Rennie decided uneasily, that some customers did come back, quite satisfied, for another animal; and many did get a good beast from the Silver Horseshoe Stables, though never cheaply, and rarely even reasonably. Joe Gallon bought astonishingly cheaply, and almost always managed to sell astonishingly dear. On the other hand, there was no doubt that some people were badly disappointed on getting their purchase back home; and when refunds and exchanges were sought, Joe could be a very awkward man. The horse had always been perfectly sound, or quiet, or gentle, on leaving him: it was always the customer who was at fault; and if an exchange was arranged it was invariably with further profit in Joe's pocket.

There was one horse in particular, a good-looking chestnut called Ginger, that came back to the stables three times in Rennie's first fortnight. He was always kept up smartly in the stables, as if ready for frequent trial and sale, and he was downright vicious and mean. Joe never let Rennie go near him in the ordinary way; but the strange thing was Ginger's total change of character when being inspected by any potential buyer. Joe would lead him out from his stall, handling him calmly and with confidence, and Rennie, expecting to see the white eyes and bared teeth that were Ginger's usual greeting, was always astonished by his gentleness on these occasions.

'A lovely, confidential hack, that,' Joe would say, looking as honest as a missionary. 'Child could handle 'im. I'll get my girl to pop into the plate and show you his paces.'

This was where Rennie would mount and take the chestnut round the paddock, while Joe and the customer stood watching by the gate. And then the customer would have a try, and all the time Ginger's manner was beyond reproach. He was so good-looking and such a beautiful mover, that a sale was almost invariably concluded. Joe never let horses out on trial. 'Now that'd be no sense, would it, madam? I don't carry insurance for all my stock and anything could happen. But I'll always consider a fair exchange, and no man can do more.'

Ginger always came back. He had been wild, vicious, unmanageable; he had pulled, bucked, kicked, and fly-jumped; he was nappy, traffic-shy, and dangerous.

'Well, you saw for yourself how he was here, madam. I mean, it makes you see why I say I'll never send 'em out on trial, doesn't it? I don't know what you did to him, to upset him so; but send him back by all means. I can't entertain a refund, of course, but I'll be only too happy to do you a suitable exchange.'

'Do you' seemed to be the key words here, Rennie thought sadly; for now that he had the customer where he wanted him, or her, Joe could fix what price he fancied on the exchange. 'I'm afraid this horse is bound to cost you a bit more: you see I got Ginger so cheap – from an old friend, you understand – that I could afford to let you have him at a favourable figure. But this horse, now, cost me a lot of money – and worth every penny. I'll get my girl to take him out for you. . . .'

Rennie smiled with a wistful amusement when Joe suddenly said, one day, after Ginger's fourth homecoming in the month; 'You know, Rennie, I don't know what I'll do without Ginger if some darn-fool fellow goes and keeps him. Brought me in hundreds, that horse; and blow me if I haven't got kind of fond of him – the old devil!'

For a long time Rennie could only suppose, in a kind of baffled wonder, that Ginger was really fond enough of Joe to behave well for him when Joe wanted. But one day, when Rennie had been at Bentley for nearly a month, there came a sudden inquiry, at the door, for a horse of Ginger's description. There was the customer, right on the threshold, asking to see any suitable animals straight away. For a moment Joe was in a bit of a fluster, but only for a moment.

'Certainly, certainly; I've got the very horse. Nice looking confidential chestnut, make a show-hack, he's got such good conformation. Now look, will you come inside and I'll get my Missis to make you a cup of tea? It'll be welcome on such a cold morning, I'm sure. Then I'll be with you in ten minutes.'

Rennie was at that time answering the telephone, and as soon as she had finished she dashed after Joe to the stables. He didn't hear her walking along the straw-scattered passage behind the stalls, and he jumped when she met him coming out of Ginger's stall. The first thing Rennie noticed was the extremely guilty look on Joe's face – but that soon melted off. The next thing she saw was a hypodermic syringe in his hand. Rennie's eyes were held by it, in a sudden horrible fascination. Ginger ... drugs ... that magic gentleness ...

'What's up, Rennie, eh? Look as if you'd seen a corpse! Just thought I give Ginny his tonic: has it for the blood, you know. Wonderful what the vets can do in these days, isn't it? ... Now, get his saddle and bridle – look slippery, lass. And, Rennie! I meant to tell you – I thought of raising your cash. Always said I would if you worked well, and you have done. Eight quid a week – and that's doubling what you started on. But I can afford it. Gives a business prestige, a good girl does. And, what's more, we needn't stop at eight. Go on doing well by me, and I'll go on doing well by you. That's fair enough, eh? And, Rennie! A bit less squeamish, and you'd suit me perfect! Can't be too soft in business, you know; especially in the horse trade. Now, buzz along and saddle him up.'

For Rennie, this was the beginning of the end. In some ways, she was sorry, because there were aspects of the Gallon establishment that she rather enjoyed. Joe himself was not entirely bad; he could be very good company, and he could be generous and kind and considerate. Mrs Gallon was a poor, meek wisp of a woman, but Rennie was fond of her in a negative sort of way; and now that she was used to it she liked the big, untidy house, full of sprawling dogs and cats, and she enjoyed the zest and pace of her daily life. The bustle and excitement of the big horse sales was heady and absorbing; and the many and varied contacts with different people and animals interested her enormously. The money, too, was almost unbelievably lavish, after years of acute economy, and Rennie was saving in quite a big way. Joe Gallon often tossed her a guinea or so as commission from some especially good sale, and she was able to save most of her weekly wages. More important than all this; her health was now so good that she began, cautiously, to think of herself as almost cured. And, heaven knew, she had enough anxiety and danger in this job to provoke a relapse, if she had still been liable to have one.

But however much there was to be said for the job, Rennie knew now that she was no longer content in it, and she began, a little half-heartedly, to look down the Situations Vacant columns in the various horsy papers that Joe Gallon regularly bought. But it was the same as when she had been looking for a job before. Everyone wanted skilled and experienced people; and Rennie had still done almost no jumping, no proper hunting, no showing and no schooling. She could not teach, and had only just begun to realize what the diagonal aids were. Also, even for skilled girls, the wages offered – when they were mentioned – were nowhere near the sum that she was now receiving from Joe Gallon. Rennie began again to drift into a 'waiting-for-an-opportunity' state of mind. She hated change, and was reluctant to think of a new upheaval, and so soon. Presently, she found herself making excuses for Joe, and even entertaining the idea that perhaps Ginger did have a tonic administered by hypodermic syringe, and so she had been unfair to Joe all the time.

Letters from home brought good news about the new job at Kingwood School, which Rennie's father had duly been offered and had taken up at the beginning of the Lent term. The old staff cottage had turned out to be quite delightful, Mr Jordan wrote – sunny and more roomy than it looked from the outside. Aunt Lucy liked it, but she had mentioned once or twice lately the possibility of going back to her job at the Remand School again, since Rennie seemed so happily established and Robin was now at Kingwood School all day. He and Robin had both been riding quite a lot, and everyone at the stables always asked about Rennie, and looked forward to seeing her in her holidays.

Sudden pangs of homesickness for Kingwood, and all its decent honestness, would assail Rennie when she read these letters and the letters from Miss Brandon and Ann; but there was no time for nostalgia in the Silver Horseshoe Stables, and Rennie soon got over these moments of sadness in the rush and excitements of the day. As February drew to its close there came a sudden spell of heavy snow and hard frosts which lasted well into March. Joe and Rennie and the two stable men spent hours of every day in lungeing the indoor horses on a cleared ring in one of the paddocks, as this was the only way to exercise them while the countryside was white and frozen. The lying-out horses looked wretched to Rennie; huddled in the snow against the hedges, always waiting for someone to bring hay and break the ice on their troughs. But Joe laughed at her for a 'softy', and said the horses didn't feel as cold as she did.

Sometimes, during this long freeze-up, Rennie would think of Miss Brandon and the money she must be losing: no hunting, rides all cancelled, and still the rent and rates and fodder and wages bills to pay. But business went on much as usual for

Joe Gallon: horses in and horses out; complaints about a cow that had been found to have mastitis ('She was perfectly all right when she left me,' said Joe) and someone else bringing back Ginger. But one day Joe over-stepped himself with Ginger, and sold him to a boy not much older than Robin. He reminded Rennie of Robin a little, too, having the same fair pinkness and exuberant confidence in life. She hated the whole of her part in the affair; the showing of Ginger's manners and paces, the studied patting of his beautiful cruel head and the imposed silence when she wanted to shout out, 'No! Don't have him!' to the boy's favourably impressed parents.

He was called Keith, and his father bought the handsome chestnut for him. 'He's a good little rider,' he told Rennie as they watched him trying Ginger round the cleared ring in the snow. 'Too good for the pony he's had up till now. I promised him a full-sized hack if he passed his grammar school entry, and we've just heard that he's got it.'

Two days later the boy was dead. Rennie knew when she heard Joe answer the telephone. 'I really am shocked, sir – deeply sorry – such a nice lad, too. Please convey my sympathy to your wife.... But I must say, I can't understand it – can't understand it at all. The horse was perfectly gentle with us; you saw for yourself....'

Rennie ran blindly out into the yard and was sick on the snow. And that night she had the first screaming nightmares since the Mermaid affair.

# 14 | The Value of Money

Rennie had not slept much that night – and neither had Joe and Mrs Gallon. Long before dawn she was awake for good, and lying wide-eyed, staring at the darkness and muddling her way through the new forest of problems that had grown up around her. She felt that if only she could make herself think clearly she would be able to see the way ahead; but whenever she managed to force her mind into facing the situation squarely, it shied off, like a frightened horse, and left her heart beating hard in near-panic, and the terrible thought of the fair-pink boy, who was dead now, and the treacherous Ginger.

When morning came she knew only one thing – that she could no longer take any part in selling horses for Joe Gallon. This would automatically mean the end of her job, since selling was the main part of it; and as her presence would now be both an annoyance to Joe and a misery to herself, she knew that she must make some kind of plans to leave as soon as possible.

There had been a time when Rennie suddenly understood the old belief in malevolent gods. On this morning, she understood the feeling of being miraculously and unexpectedly favoured. At breakfast, opening a letter from her father, she began to read it almost absent-mindedly: news of Robin and the school and Aunt Lucy – really leaving in the summer, it seemed – and answers to Rennie's own questions: then suddenly her attention was arrested:

'By the way, has Ann told you about Maurice Lowe? I must

say that there is a strange young man. A fall from the chestnut Barbemusche seems to have had the dramatic effect of restoring his joggled mind to exactly what it was before his first accident; not only has all his old riding skill come back to him, but also the serene conviction that first love is to be last love. I hear that Sally yesterday announced their engagement. So that really it was just as well that you were not impressed, yourself! One happy thing that this event does bring about, of course, is the end of your self-imposed banishment from Kingwood. But I don't expect you will jump for joy at this, considering your present state of prosperity!'

For a long time Rennie could not read the rest of this letter, but just stared at it without taking in any more words.

'You've got a mighty long billy-doo,' said Joe a little suspiciously. 'And not eating your breakfast, either. I must say I hope you're not sickening for anything. Delirious all night and sick yesterday, and no appetite now....'

'Joe, I'm going home today.' Oddly enough, her voice sounded perfectly calm to herself – it even sounded content.

'Going *home*? But look here, Rennie, I mean to *say*.... It's all very well flying into a bit of temperament over the little feller's accident – I felt bad enough, myself – but you can't let things like that knock you sideways.... Well, I mean to say!' Joe went on for some minutes, alternately furious and persuading.

But Rennie said nothing at all, except that she was sorry, because she knew that there was nothing else to say.

She sent a telegram home: 'Have jumped for joy. Expect me this evening. Explain all then. Love, Rennie.'

Ethel Gallon wept a little, in her subdued way, when Rennie said good-bye, but Joe just looked outraged and bewildered, as one who never could understand the ways of women. He drove Rennie to the station, though, in his elegant brake, with the determination of one who means to do right by someone who is letting him down; and he sent her off with a characteristic string of platitudes about giving and taking, and every man for himself, and the rough with the smooth.

'I'm sorry, Joe,' Rennie said again. 'There were lots of things I enjoyed very much, but it simply isn't my kind of life.'

All the way home she watched the flying white countryside, listening to the galloping noise of the train-wheels and thinking, 'So many miles nearer home, and Kingwood.' The terrible things of her life, that she had always seemed to be running away from, came slowly through her mind in turn as the journey hammered on: the bombing, the car crash, Templar, Mermaid, Dark Stranger, and now Keith; but in some way they were no longer terrible, to be shoved down in dark corners of the mind. They were simply a part of life – perhaps of anyone's life – and gradually one learned to accept them, for the part they were in the scheme of things. She had learned a lot since she left school, Rennie reflected, remembering how she had once felt younger than her years, whereas now she felt so much older.

In the late afternoon the familiar Hampshire countryside was gliding past the carriage windows, and Rennie looked at it affectionately, as if each snow-covered tree and field were in some way a part of home. And then, at Charterhill Station, she recognized Miss Brandon on the platform.

'I heard you were coming home, and as I had to be in Charterhill to fetch some mended tack, I thought I'd see if you were on this train. I've got Amelia outside. Oh, it is nice to see you again!'

Wedged inside Amelia among two saddles, three bridles, and half a sack of layers' mash, Rennie really began to feel at home.

'Such a good-hearted car,' Miss Brandon was saying as they drove up through the hilly little town. 'I thought she seemed to be getting a bit tired on the hills last week, and I took her into the garage for vetting while I was shopping this afternoon. They put her right, as you can see by our coming up here in top, but Mr Jenkins said she was in such a state, he wondered how she really went at all. But she never gives up; and if she must go wrong she always goes wrong near to home.'

Rennie smiled with a tired kind of happiness. 'How is everybody? I can't tell you how often I've thought of you all, and wished I was back.'

'Well, Sally's very happy, of course. She'll be leaving us at Easter to be married. Maurice's riding memory began to come back in leaps and bounds after a fall he had off Barbemusche, which must have shaken the odd bits of his mind back again, I suppose. After a bit we stopped pretending to teach him any more. He talks of riding in point-to-points again this spring, if the snow ever clears enough to have them.'

'And Mermaid? Is she really as well as everyone said in their letters?'

'I think so,' said Miss Brandon. 'We haven't hunted her, of course, but we're hacking her – or we were before the freeze-up. She's really made rather a miraculous recovery. We didn't tell you, but she had a third operation while you were away. Mr Simpson was wonderful with her. He said she had such courage that he just wouldn't let her die. Of course, we all thought that she would never let anyone bridle her again, after all this, but she doesn't seem to be touchy about her head at all.'

'Unlike Jester,' said Rennie reminiscently.

'Who, so far as anyone knows, has no reason to feel touchy,' Miss Brandon agreed.

'Has the freeze-up been really terrible?'

Miss Brandon thought for a moment, nursing Amelia over the crest of a hill. 'Well, from the money point of view it's been pretty bad. Luckily, my hay man doesn't worry me. . . . And of course there's been a lot of extra work, lungeing the horses in the snow, and clearing tracks and all that. I must say, Robin and your father have been a great stand-by. They really seemed to enjoy helping us all, and Robin is getting quite good. I'm very pleased about him, because nowadays it's nearly always girls; the boys seem to have little real interest in riding, on the whole.'

Rennie said, 'I'm glad about Dad and Robin, too, but I'm terribly sorry about the money.'

'Oh, well,' said Miss Brandon philosophically, 'when you take up riding as a career, you know that you must expect hard winters from time to time, and that they will always be a dead loss. It simply isn't the job for anyone who feels that money is very important.'

'There's a horrid fascination about money,' Rennie said; 'seeing it coming in, and saving it, and thinking of all that one can do with it. But that's all gone dead on me. Just now, I think it's the least important thing in the whole of life. I shan't care if I never earn more than my bare needs, ever again.'

'It doesn't do to belittle the value of money,' said Miss Brandon sensibly. 'But all the same, I do agree that it's really one of the lesser things, and nowhere near as important as being happy in your job, for instance.'

Rennie said, 'It's funny, but in spite of all the things that happened to me in my job with you, I've never been so really happy, before or since.'

'It's still open to you,' said Miss Brandon. 'I shall have to have someone when Sally goes, and I'd sooner it were you for more reasons than one.' She turned Amelia into the home lane.

'What sort of reasons?' Rennie was curious.

'I expect they'll reveal themselves to you, in time,' said Miss Brandon enigmatically.

'I'd love to have the job!'

'What! No questions about money?' Miss Brandon smiled.

'No. I'm a bit sick of the idea of money. I leave it to you.'

'I can only start you with thirty bob: I'm nearly broke, just after the frost. But I'll put it up to two pounds as soon as I can.'

'I don't think I really care!' said Rennie; and then the roofs of Kingwood Stables came in sight above the bare trees, and to Rennie it was the same as the towers of Samarkand to weary travellers seeking it. 'Home again!' she said, 'and a sort of double home to me, now, with Dad and Robin and Aunt Lucy just beyond us, too. I used to think that everything horrible happened to me, but now it's everything perfect. Make Amelia gallop, Miss B! I can't wait to be there. Does Hallmark still drink sugary tea? And Barbemusche look embittered in his box? And Puffin slip away from her pups? And Snowy run up to people's shoulders? And is the chaff-cutter still dealing out lumbago? And does the stove-pipe in the tack-room still have to be banged to make it "draw"?'

Miss Brandon laughed. 'Everything is as you say, I'm afraid, except that Puffin's pups have long since grown up and gone away. And we're still always late for Mrs Waddy's lunches, and poor Mandy still wants a stray dog more than anything else. Unfortunately, she found one this morning. Being a Saturday she was here as usual, of course, and we were hacking round the few cleared roads, and went past the old gipsy-camp site, on the common you know. They'd suddenly gone but there was a very scruffy-looking mongrel hanging round in the snow. Mandy badly wanted to take it home with her at once, but we felt she really oughtn't to, and dissuaded her. After all, we weren't sure it was abandoned, and it might even have been dangerous.'

'Poor Mandy! She's very single-minded, for her age.'

'Much the same as you were, about horses,' said Miss Brandon.

'Yes, I suppose so,' Rennie said, and then added teasingly as the car nosed in beside Shamus's little tub-cart, 'Amelia knows her own way into her stable! Do you rug her up, in this cold weather?'

'Well really, I do,' admitted Miss Brandon. 'But I haven't yet come to putting condition powders in her petrol!' She switched off the engine and opened the door. 'Here you are; home again at last: I don't know why, and I'm not going to ask, but you're downright welcome, whatever it was.'

'I'll tell you when I can bear to think about it,' Rennie said.

'There's Robin and your father!' said Miss Brandon, and Rennie shot out of the car. Then there was Ann, and Aunt Lucy too; and Sally, being as welcoming and friendly as if Rennie had never gone half across England for her sake; and then the cats and Puffin were all around her; and Robin was shouting above his father's and Aunt Lucy's welcomes to explain where he had got in his riding.

'It only lacks Tom and Mrs Waddy!' Rennie said happily.

'Tom's in the tack-room,' said Ann. 'He said he'd let the others get their stuff over first.'

'We can even supply Mrs Waddy!' said Sally.

'Well you see, when we got your telegram,' said Mr Jordan, 'we thought we'd all have supper together.'

'So I stayed on,' said Ann.

'And they wouldn't let me cook it at the cottage,' complained Aunt Lucy.

'Because Mrs Waddy wanted to stay and do it,' explained Miss Brandon kindly, 'and the stable flat is bigger, for such a crowd.'

'And I'm staying up for it,' said Robin, 'and Tom's coming, too. But he took an awful lot of persuading because of having his working-clothes on.'

Rennie laughed, and then suddenly said solemnly, 'It only needs one thing to make it perfect. I do hope Mrs Waddy has brought the photographs of all her grandchildren!'

'I expect she has,' said Sally, opening the little gate. 'Her daughter's had twins since you left!'

# 15 | A Part of the Planning

ALMOST as if there had been no break at all, Rennie took up her work at Kingwood again; but now she found it more enjoyable than ever before, in contrast to the life and principles at the Silver Horseshoe Stables.

The only real difference was that she was now living at home, with her wages adjusted accordingly, because of home being only half a paddock away and Robin and her father anxious to have her with them again. Aunt Lucy, too, was pleased to have her at home, but she was now in a thinking-ahead state of mind, planning and talking about her approaching return to her job. 'You'll have to fit in what housekeeping you can, before and after stables,' she said at breakfast the first morning, and then added enigmatically, 'unless I'm right about which way the wind is blowing.'

'What wind?' asked Robin, eating hurriedly so that there would be time to dash over the melting snow and help with the ponies before church.

Mr Jordan suddenly looked up from his porridge, grinning both broadly and sheepishly. 'Well, I don't see why everyone shouldn't know, really, since nearly everyone seems to have found out by simple observation. I must say, it does show how transparent is the average human mind.'

'Dad—?' Rennie stared at him with wide, querying eyes, and Robin suddenly grinned too.

'Oh, that!' he said. 'If you mean about you and Miss B, that's old stuff. Everyone saw through it years ago, Dad, only we didn't like to say so, as you seemed to fancy keeping it secret.'

'Dad – really?' Rennie could hardly take in these astonishing innuendos.

Mr Jordan looked bashfully at his spoon. 'Well – I – yes, of course it's true. Jean and I are secretly engaged.'

'Secretly!' said Robin, with a sudden snort of laughter.

'Well, not secretly any longer,' admitted his father. 'Or probably never at all, from all I hear. We wanted to keep it secret until we were quite sure what you and Rennie felt about it, old chap. I mean, it didn't seem right to us to provide you both with a step-mother whether you liked the idea or not. And we thought that if you hated it, we need never publish the idea at all.'

Robin gave a loud delighted guffaw. 'Dear old Dad! It must have published itself. Well, if you want to know what I think, I'm jolly well all in favour. Everyone else at school has a mother, except me, but Miss B's nicer than all the ones that turned up at the school play.'

'And what about you, Rennie?'

'Oh, Dad, I simply can't imagine anything more absolutely right! And I think Mother would think so, too; she wasn't the kind that would want to be remembered by an emptiness. But, the funny thing is, the possibility of it never even occurred to me!'

'That's the trouble with all you growing children,' said Aunt Lucy with a sniff. 'You never think of your parents and uncles and aunts as being still human and really quite young. You think that no one over thirty can ever have exciting and worrying lives, or fall in love, or wonder what to do for the best.'

'Where are we all going to live? Here in this cottage, or over the stables?' Rennie asked, her eyes shining.

'Good gracious, we haven't thought as far as that. Over the stables, I should imagine.'

'It's like trying to choose between, say, health and happiness!

This cottage is so nice, but living over the stables would be wonderful. And Miss B won't want to give up the horses.'

'Neither of us want to give them up,' said Mr Jordan. 'You may laugh to think of me riding, but I'm not so bad! I can rise to the trot and sit down to the canter, and Jean says she's seen worse hands.'

'Really, of course, she needs a man about the place,' said Aunt Lucy, beginning to clear the breakfast-table, 'to help her with the accounts, and lifting heavy sacks, and things like that.'

'But, Lucy dear, that's not why I'm marrying her,' said Mr Jordan, with his mouth kinking up at the corners.

No one went riding that afternoon because of the slippery state of the thawing snow – no-one but Mandy and Robin, that is, and nothing would have stopped them from riding on a Sunday afternoon, with five days of school in a bleak chain ahead of them. Mandy's pony, Acorn, had developed a girth-gall, as even the best-managed ponies sometimes will, and could not be saddled, so that Mandy was riding him bareback.

'But yesterday it felt like riding on a roof-ridge – he has a kind of dorsal fin where his spine ought to be – so I've got six pairs of school pants on today.'

Miss Brandon made them both promise to keep to the cleared roads, and they rode off in the north-east wind, full of purpose.

'I'm afraid Mandy has the gipsy mongrel on her mind,' she said, watching them go. 'I wish she didn't mind so badly about homeless dogs.'

Rennie and Sally barrowed hay to the ponies in the fields, the wheels and their gumboots slithering in the slush. But there were missel-thrushes singing in the trees around the stables, and the wind was gradually backing.

Mandy and Robin rode in earlier than usual, and Mandy was without her coat, though the wind was still sharp. Closer observation by Rennie and Miss Brandon, in the tack-room doorway, revealed the coat wrapped round a small, bulky object that she was carrying in front of her as she rode.

'Mandy! That's not the gipsy mongrel!' But Miss Brandon knew it was.

'Look!' Mandy opened a crack of her coat very tenderly, as Acorn stopped at the doorway and stretched his neck in a home-again-at-last manner.

'It was still there,' Robin explained, 'shivering round the encampment place, in all the snow and slush.'

'We couldn't have left him,' said Mandy.

She dropped her reins on Acorn's neck and slithered carefully to the ground, holding the dog tightly. 'He's quite the most homeless dog that any dog could be. And in all that snow, Miss B.'

'What if your mother says no, or if the gipsies come back and claim him?' Miss Brandon was anxious that Mandy's hopes should not be raised too high, if they must only be dashed down again. But Robin said, 'Of course we can't help it if the gipsies come back – but we're sure they won't, or they'd never have abandoned him. And if Mandy isn't allowed to keep him, I knew Dad would let me have him at the cottage, and he could really be Mandy's all the time. I shouldn't mind, because after you've married Dad I shall be sort of part-owner of Puffin and all the puppies she ever has, as well as all the cats, and – oh, gosh! – even the horses and ponies, I suppose!' he added in an awed voice, as the thought suddenly struck him. 'I say, Miss B, when had you thought of having the wedding?'

Later in the week, but long before the weekend, Mandy came to the stables straight from school one afternoon, to bring the glorious news. 'Mummy said I could! And he's called Gipsy, and we think he's part Cairn. Mummy said we must tell the police, but they said they'd had no inquiries, and now we've got the licence. Do you know, he wouldn't eat out of a plate, but only from our hands? I suppose they just used to throw him a crust. He was really the most waif-and-stray kind of dog that anyone could have; don't you think so, Miss B?'

'Now you'll be able to go riding with a dog at your heels!'

said Tom, who was starting on the pile of tack from a hunting day.

'I know! And Mother says it doesn't really matter about getting home in daylight any more, now that I've got Gipsy to look after me.'

With the first swing-round of the wind to a milder quarter, spring really began to burst out in the south country. While snow and hard frost still lay in the shadowed places, everywhere else seemed suddenly greener and golder and bluer. The horses and ponies began casting their coats, Sally found a broody hen in a pony-box, pussy-willow tufts opened like little powder-puffs along the branches, and the Easter Holidays were near enough for Robin to start chanting, 'This time next week, where shall I be?'

There was much talk of weddings in the stables, although Miss Brandon didn't forget herself so far as to overlook the plans for holiday riding events. There was to be a gymkhana for all the children, and tea-ride at least once a week. Tea-rides were very popular with all ages, and were Miss Brandon's speciality. Some distant village inn would be chosen where tea was arranged in advance, and Miss Brandon would work out different cross-country routes for the outward journey and the return.

'But I can't possibly get married in my busiest season!' she would say to Rennie's father when he suggested that there were other things to plan as well as tea-rides and gymkhanas. 'It's like asking a farmer to get married in the middle of haymaking.'

Sally and Ann took out the last junior boys' class of the term, and the next day Rennie and Miss Brandon took out the last class of seniors. Rennie was as happy as human kind well can be. She was on Mermaid, who seemed as well as ever she had been in the old days, and the snow had all finally gone, and the sun was shining through air that came straight from the warm south, heavy with borrowed summer.

Morgan Davy came riding up beside her on the broad path over the common, and presently they were deep in the planning of Morgan's farm again, just as they always were before the long, strange days with Joe Gallon.

'I don't really know about sheep,' Morgan was saying. 'I'd like to keep sheep: I think they really pay if they're well managed; but they are rather a specialized line. They have all sorts of diseases that no other animal has, and they need to be always watched and cared for, or they'll just lie down and die, as easy as that.'

Rennie said, 'I think, really, that the future for farming in England is in dairying and poultry. After all, eggs and milk are the two things that no foreign country can possibly compete with, because they're only nice when they're really fresh.'

'I've sometimes thought about New Zealand,' Morgan said thoughtfully. 'Don't you sometimes feel sort of cramped for room in little England? I know I do.'

Rennie laughed. 'I suppose I might do, one day. But, just now, I can't imagine any place in all the world that could be as nice as Kingwood Stables.'

'Oh, well, they're all right, of course,' said Morgan grudgingly. 'Only at present there's not much sense in anyone there, excepting you. All this endless talk of weddings.'

'It's only a temporary condition,' said Rennie apologetically, but with a sudden twinkle. 'After all, I suppose that when you get married you do think it's rather important.'

'I've sometimes thought,' said Morgan reflectively, 'that when we're old enough, say in three or four years, it wouldn't be a bad idea for us to get married, too.'

Rennie said nothing for a moment, looking absently at Mermaid's ears and thinking how odd it was that, though they were both nearly eighteen, she felt almost completely grown-up now, while Morgan was still obviously a schoolboy. But, as he said, it wouldn't be a bad idea at all, when one came to think about it.

'After all,' Morgan said, 'we do get on awfully well. I missed you quite a lot when you were away. And I can't imagine anyone else at all on my farm, except you. I mean, you really are interested in it. And in horses, too. You know, I think we might have a lot of fun.'

'I daresay you're right,' said Rennie, with a sudden grin at him. 'Let's make it a part of the planning.'